Women
of the Third World

Women
of the Third World

Work and Daily Life

Jeanne Bisilliat

AND

Michèle Fiéloux

TRANSLATED BY

Enne Amann and Peter Amann

Rutherford • Madison • Teaneck
Fairleigh Dickinson University Press
London and Toronto: Associated University Presses

Associated University Presses
440 Forsgate Drive
Cranbury, NJ 08512

Associated University Presses
25 Sicilian Avenue
London WC1A 2QH, England

Associated University Presses
2133 Royal Windsor Drive
Unit 1
Mississauga, Ontario
Canada L5J 1K5

The paper used in this publication meets the requirements
of the American National Standard for Permanence of Paper
for Printed Library Materials Z39.48-1984.

Library of Congress Cataloging-in-Publication Data

Bisilliat, Jeanne.
  Women of the Third World.

  Translation of: Femmes du Tiers-monde.
  Bibliography: p.
  Includes index.
  1. Women in development—Developing countries.
  2. Women—Developing countries—Economic conditions.
  3. Women—Employment—Developing countries. I. Fiéloux,
Michèle. II. Title.
HQ1249.5.D44B5713 1987   305.4'09172'4   86-46328
ISBN 0–8386–3311–0 (alk. paper)

Contents

Preface to the American Edition

WE WOULD LIKE, FIRST OF ALL, TO EXPRESS OUR PLEASURE AT SEEING our book published in the United States. We also want to thank our translators, Peter and Enne Amann, not only for their excellent translation of this study, but for all their efforts in behalf of its publication. Finally, we extend our warmest thanks to Fairleigh Dickinson University Press, which agreed to publish our work. As far as the scholarly field of women and development is concerned, this seems to be the first time that a book written by French women researchers has been translated and published in English. Whatever the differences between our respective countries, we welcome what we see as the convergence of our interests.

Women of the Third World was completed in November 1982 and, as we mentioned in our introduction, it was influenced by the state of research at that point in the decade. All scholarly study is conditioned by its own moment in time. If we had to re-write the book today, we would retain the same objectives, but advances made in urban research since 1982 would allow us to modify the relevant chapters.

It is evident that in recent years, research on women in an urban setting has developed a good deal all over the world. This has also applied to France, but it has been especially true for Latin America, where the growing metropolitan areas constitute a rich area for study. In fact, this type of research permits us not only to understand more fully the phenomena of urbanization, but also the special strategies for survival that women employ, whether they belong to a traditional family (in the normal, restrictive sense of the word) or to a single-parent family. By its very scope, the increase in the number of women heading households has become a focus of special attention. The study of this phenomenon broadens our reflections and theories dealing not only with the evolving notion of what constitutes a family, but also our perception of other concurrent important social, cultural, and economic changes.

We should, for example, clarify the link between the urban poverty of single women and the increasingly visible emergence of youth gangs, who, by becoming the primary means of socialization for their members, promote a withdrawal from society and a frightening level of delinquency. This is a real challenge thrown out to our deluded good consciences and to our too often illusory grasp of human phenomena. The continued survival of social groups is inexorably tied to the past, present, and future. These children, left to their own devices, attest to a social disequilibrium never known on such a scale, a disequilibrium that will only be understood if we put it into a global perspective.

Furthermore, nowadays widespread efforts in the domain of statistics have resulted in the use of figures that are somewhat more complete, more reliable, and more consistent. We can now easily obtain publications from agencies of the United Nations and the U. S. Census Bureau in which figures are presented with some critical perspective.

In conclusion, it seems to us that, structurally speaking, the major trends described in this book are still at work and are perhaps growing even stronger in response to the continuing, interacting crises disrupting the world, that, in turn, impinge upon national policies.

Yet a profound change is taking place. This is the onset of a revolution, which, if it matures, will be the most important since the beginning of our world: women in Asia, Latin America, and Africa are becoming increasingly aware of their exploitation by others and their economic and cultural subordination. Increasingly, from the grassroots to the top, they are organizing and insisting on having their liberties as human beings understood, recognized, and accepted.

> Whoever is a man comes with me.
> Whoever is a woman stays behind and weeps.

Little by little, these words from a song by the Brazilian Geraldo Vandre will gradually blur and fade away. Such is the hope and the expectation of all the world's women.

Paris, August 1986   Jeanne Bisilliat

Introduction: The Exclusion of Women from Development

WOMEN MAKE UP ONE-HALF OF THE WORLD'S POPULATION. THEY supply two-thirds of the labor-time of humanity, but receive only one-tenth of the total income and own less than one-hundredth of the world's goods.

The startling incongruities of these figures explain the great silence that surrounded women of the Third World until 1975, when the United Nations–sponsored Mexico City Conference inaugurated the "Year of the Woman." At that point, studies that women had already started some years earlier received a vigorous boost. In almost every country, whether developed or still developing, groups of women scholars—sociologists, economists, anthropologists—joined to establish research programs. The various specialized agencies of the United Nations followed up by insisting that in dealing with problems of development, the social and economic role of women should henceforth receive the attention it deserved. In the future, women were to be put on the agenda of world conferences focusing on essential needs such as employment or land reform. Modest funding was also provided for development projects affecting women in the areas of agriculture, handicrafts, and industry. This difficult undertaking came up against many obstacles, the most important of which was indifference or incredulity on the part of the men in charge. Allowing women to enter a domain as basic as the economic development of the Third World often still may seem incongruous.

Anyone interested in the place of women in the Third World faces the problem of a documentation that is scattered, difficult to obtain, incomplete, and disorganized. Nonetheless, the woman of the Third World is not some unknowable residue. She does exist. It is this woman that we have wanted to meet.

We have followed her in three large regions: Latin America, Africa, and Asia. To do this, we made a threefold choice. First, because they are the most numerous, we have focused on women belonging to the most disadvantaged social strata, living below the poverty level. Second, we chose a particular theme, that of work in the countryside and in the city. For these women, labor determines their life, or, more exactly, their survival. Third, we chose those areas of the Third World that have been fully drawn into the capitalist world economy. This is why, for instance, we shall encounter examples from South Korea, but not from a North Korea that has remained relatively insulated from the world economy. This is not to say that collectivist planned economies may not have their own problems of poverty, discrimination, and even exploitation.

Our aim has been to provide a description of women's economic role in the Third World, rather than a history or theory of female employment. Indeed, one has to begin this task by identifying women's work and rescuing it from almost complete invisibility. We have focused on the mechanism by which women's labor is inexorably drawn into an international market based on the division of labor. The similarity of the conditions and forms of employment for women seem to be a common denominator which groups the poor women of the capitalist world into a homogeneous group.

To acknowledge choices is to admit gaps. We have deliberately excluded the cultural elements that explain the differences in the adaptation of social groups to new economic conditions. In our opinion, though each specific culture may adjust in its own way to change, it is powerless to check the irresistible forces that, everywhere, reduce countries and peoples to dependence. Our book, therefore, seeks to reveal a reality that is normally hidden. In discussions of underdevelopment women have often gone unmentioned, as though they were not part of the problem. Our book is intended to make up for this omission.

The facts have led us to establish specific links between type of work and a particular region: paid farm work in Latin America; factory work in Southeast Asia; women peasants in Africa. We have tried to show that the same type of work may exist elsewhere on a more limited scale, but within the same framework. The choice of our examples has always been guided by the same principles: to show as clearly as possible how the work of women is essential to the survival of the poor. We have also tried to show that the exploitation of women's labor threatens the very existence of the poor.

Women
of the Third World

1

A World of Inequalities

EVERYONE IS AWARE THAT THE THIRD WORLD HAS EXPERIENCED A dramatic increase in poverty that, paradoxically, accompanies a certain kind of economic growth. The whole conceptual and statistical arsenal that has been elaborated these last years to measure poverty (the threshold of poverty, the threshold of absolute poverty, and the minimum caloric and protein intake) in the end obscures the fact that poverty and destitution are not only abstract categories but the ills that weigh down men, women, and children. Very often this also obscures a terribly simple reality: within the most impoverished groups, there is a hierarchy that accounts for the greater suffering of women and children. "Is anyone more underfed and more desperate than a poor man at the lowest rung of the social ladder in an underdeveloped country?" The answer is, "Yes, his wife and, most often, his children" (George 1978).

The structural reasons for poverty—economic, social, political, psychological—converge to accentuate this inequality within inequality. It seems more and more urgent to show how women, together with men, but in different ways, are caught up in the great destabilizing phenomena of the world economy and, specifically, how their labor is systematically exploited.

We will examine poverty in the rural zones where it predominates. Actually, the greater part of the Third World population is still rural: 63 percent in Asia, 69 percent in Africa, 47 percent in Central America, and 39 percent in South America (Jalé 1973).

The real poor, those who suffer from malnutrition and who have an annual income of less than $50 (700 million in 1972), live mainly in the rural areas, and 70 percent of these are in Asia. These are the small-holding peasants, the sharecroppers, the landless peasants, and the temporary farm workers. In eight Asiatic countries, poverty is increasing (Ghai et al. 1979) and in seven of those, the proportion of the population living under the poverty threshold was greater in 1980 than in 1970: 78 percent in Bangladesh, where the proportion of the poorest was multiplied

13

by five. In Latin America, 90.8 million, that is, 58 percent of the
population, live below the poverty threshold. In Africa, even
though data are harder to come by, they lead to the same conclusion: 51 percent of the population in northern Nigeria, 88
percent in Kenya and Tanzania and 91 percent in Lesotho are
poor.

Why does this situation exist? Why is there this tidal wave of
misery and hunger in the wake of our consumer societies?

The writings on hunger, on food as a weapon, have multiplied
since the famine that struck the Sahelian countries of West Africa
in 1972 and catalyzed ideas about development. A concensus is
emerging, eliminating certain accepted ideas that used to comfort
our consciences.

Hunger in the world can no longer be blamed merely on
natural calamities. The famine of 1943 in Bengal coexisted with a
level of food production 9 percent higher than that of 1941;
famine developed in a province in Ethiopia in 1973, when the
agricultural production of the country was comparable to its best
years; famine broke out in Bangladesh in 1974, when the avail-
ability of food had never been as high (Institut Tricontinental
1982). Yet natural disasters may converge to increase famine
wherever the organization of society allows, in the case of a slight
drop in production, a reduction in seed available for the following
harvest and the hoarding and speculation on the part of the grain
merchants and local tradesmen—in short, a rise in food prices. In
spite of losses (due to the floods of 1974), it is estimated that there
were four million tons of rice in Bangladesh . . . but the great
majority of people, living in destitution and having been hit hard
by the floods, were too poor to be able to buy rice; rice became
contraband in India, where it was sold for at least twice the usual
price. In Bangladesh itself, speculators sold rice for at least fifty
cents a pound in a country where the annual per capita income
was $70. Prices of other foodstuffs were inflated by 200 to 500
percent (Raymer 1975). These are examples of price manipula-
tion that starve the poorest people. The worldwide stocks of rice
tripled between 1965 and 1970. Prices began to decline, which
brought about a decrease in investments and areas planted, even
in developing countries: a ton of rice valued at $129 in 1971 rose
to $630 in April 1974.

Neither is population growth responsible for hunger. The
problem is one of distribution. The increasing number of poor
people in no way condemns them to die of hunger. The problem
is one of redistribution, of social structure. Thus, in recent years,

the world produced 1,300 million tons of cereal, of which the developed countries consumed a good half, even though they represent only one-fourth of the world's population. Their animals eat "the equivalent of all human consumption in China and India combined" (about 1 billion 300 million persons). And, when cereal stocks become too high, certain governments withdraw millions of acres from production by giving subsidies to farmers (for example, the U.S. withdrew 49,420,000 acres in 1973.) Millions of acres are given over to so-called food production, even though such crops do not provide the daily food for local people. In northeastern Brazil, the growing of sugar cane is being greatly extended to transform it into fuel. "Sugar is going to eliminate whatever remains of subsistence crops. Hunger in the northeast will fuel the automobiles of the whole country" (Linhart 1982). A rate of increase in the population of 2.9 percent and of the gross national product of 6.3 percent (in Brazil from 1965–1974) can go hand in hand with great poverty. During the same period, in the United States, the population grew at the rate of 1.3 percent while the gross national product grew by 2 percent.

Poverty has its roots in a series of social and economic imbalances. It is, first, a perversion of agricultural production systems introduced by the colonial powers that leads to a systematic pillage of the Third World; the occupation of fertile land by immense plantations of tea, of coffee for *our* consumption, of rubber and cotton for *our* factories, of soybeans and cassava for *our* livestock. Since the nineteenth century, the poor countries have been forced to produce food and agricultural raw materials destined for export, to the detriment of producing food for themselves. During the years of drought in Mali, peanut production for export rose by 25 percent and the harvest of cotton tripled, while local food crops decreased by 40 percent. Additionally, poor countries cannot pay for necessary imported food products with what they receive from the products they market, because of the growing deterioration of the terms of exchange. With 25 tons of rubber, an exporting African country that could buy six tractors in 1960 could buy only two in 1970.

This first inequality carries another with it in the way land is distributed; 2.5 percent of the landowners control about three-quarters of the cultivable land in the world (Food and Agricultural Organization 1960), and this concentration continues to grow. Six Salvadorean families owned 164,912 acres in 1961, the equivalent of the acreage owned by 107,000 families having less than 2.5 acres. The number of these families increased to 139,000 in 1974.

Their income decreased from 1,252 to 1,003 *colones* and their area of productive land decreased from 1.48 to 1.24 acres. In India, 10 percent of the landowners control half of the land; in Pakistan, 50 percent of the farmers cultivate only 10 percent of the land (Moore-Lappé and Collins 1977).

Then again, one-third of the active rural population in the Third World owns no land at all, according to World Bank statistics. Ten million workers need land in northeastern Brazil, where large landowners control 80 percent of the land. This concentration of land—an ancient phenomenon in Asia and in Latin America—continues to increase under the pressure of large property owners and the establishment of agro-business and of multinational companies. In Java since the beginning of the twentieth century, the category of those without land has increased by 30 million and in Pakistan the increase has been 350 percent between 1951 and 1961 (Ghai et al. 1979).

This concentration of land ownership makes the rich richer and the poor poorer. The latter, in turn, have incomes insufficient to assure their families' survival. In Latin America, at the beginning of the 1970s, 34 percent of the rural households did not have enough income for food (Altamir 1978). At the same time, the peasant population without land or installed on *minifundia*, tiny landholdings, represented 85 percent of the rural families in Bolivia and Guatemala, 75 percent in Ecuador and Peru, 61 percent in Columbia, and 60 percent in Mexico. This situation brings about higher and higher underemployment; this trend is accentuated by the growth in the rural population, the development of the plantation economy, and the mechanization of agriculture which increase the number of seasonal workers at the expense of permanent workers. For example, in Brazil, a tragic gap has opened between the limited demand for labor and the much larger supply of labor. Calculated by the Ministry of Agriculture in 1978, the oversupply of workers reaches 60.1 percent in the central western area, 51.2 percent in the northeast, and 63 percent in the southeast. One cannot be surprised when the nutritionist, Nelson Chaves of Pernambuco, writes: "Hunger is the most significant illness with which we have to deal. Seventy percent of the children of the state of Pernambuco suffer from malnutrition . . ." With the disappearance of the *rocas* (little plots of land allotted to the peasants as remuneration in kind, so that they can grow their own food crops), and with the large factories and sugar cane monoculture for export, "the scourge of a monotonous nutrition has been forced on the population. Now one sees sugar cane right up to the cities and the peasants no longer see any other food than black beans, manioc, and, rarely, dried meat. No fish, no milk, no vitamins . . . The average height of the peasants is diminishing. We are heading toward a generation of dwarfs" (Linhart 1982).

This spoliation of land and lowering of incomes calls into question not only the responsibility of the countries of the northern hemisphere, but also of the ruling classes of the Third World. The rich align themselves with the rich against the poor, thus setting up a most powerful transnational enterprise, even though it has no official standing. "It is the aid of the North (the developed countries) to the dominant classes and to the governments of the Third World, which contributes to the maintenance of the unequal social status quo" (Institut Tricontinental 1982).

The failure of almost all land reform programs—intended to redistribute land to those who actually till it—perpetuates conditions in which the overconsumption of some—in our own countries as well as in the Third World—depends on the underconsumption of others. The coupled growth of the economy along with poverty and malnutrition poses a problem that only social programs can resolve. That was the objective of agrarian reform. But governments are not inclined to realize radical land reform that could slow the pace of the industrialization to which they give priority. This commitment determines the direction of agricultural development, intended both to provide food for export and cheap food for growing urban centers. "The more the food situation deteriorates, the more the governments tend to turn away from land reform to find more rapid means of increasing agricultural production, that is to say, especially by technological means and by financial assistance . . . which favors the privileged classes of the village" (Les Cahiers Français 1974). The failure of the agrarian socialism of Lazaro Cardenas of Mexico in the face of industrial capitalism furnishes an enlightening example. His ouster led to the dismantling of his reforms; the communal lands of the *ejidos* (collectively owned village lands), which had increased by 7,413,000 acres, went from 40 percent down to 17 percent of the agricultural area; irrigated lands are almost exclusively controlled by rich private owners, and 16 percent of the rural work force has emigrated to the cities (Alcantara 1976).

The failure of the Green Revolution (the attempt to increase food supplies in the Third World by developing highly productive strains of grain requiring intensive use of fertilizers and chemicals and often calling for irrigation) has become obvious. In Asia, for instance, the rich farmers have seized control of credit for funding the costly new technologies. Faced with this unequal competition, the poor have become poorer. They have had to rent their land or to sell it, because land prices have increased spectacularly. They have also had to take on jobs as farm workers for lower and lower wages and with less and less steady employment. In Pakistan the mechanization of farms of twenty-five acres or more has brought about the displacement of 600,000–700,000 workers within fifteen years (Moore-Lappé and Collins 1977). The low salaries permit even fewer to survive, for due to the modernization of agriculture, the marketable surplus of cereals produced is sold at prices too high to meet domestic food needs, aside from those of the affluent groups in the cities. If the Green Revolution does permit extremely profitable investments for the multinationals (fertilizer, pesticides, equipment), it does not constitute, in any case, an answer to hunger in the world. "In the present system, these peasants have the unenviable choice of working in the city, getting into debt, or going hungry" (George 1976).

Finally, one other phenomenon works towards the deterioration of the peasants' situation: the establishment of agro-industrial complexes in the Third World. Not only do they have a powerful and negative effect on food habits—we only have to think of the success of Coca-Cola and Nestlé's milk—but where profit is law, they play a part in the diversion of natural resources. It is more profitable to devote two acres to the growing of carnations bringing in a million pesos each year than to the cultivation of wheat or corn that brings in only 12,500 pesos. It is also more profitable for General Foods or Quaker Oats to transform fish flour into a mash destined for sixty million American dogs and cats than to provide food for people.

The fact is that shortages and hunger further the interests of great powers. Hunger has already been used as a weapon. The worst error would be to underestimate the cynicism of those who define the politics of scarcity. S. George cites some instances in her book: "Food is a weapon. Today it is one of the principal tools of our diplomacy" (Earl Butz). The "ethics of the lifeboat," which consist of throwing several people overboard to prevent everyone from sinking, is supported by Dr. Garret Hardin of the University of California and several others. "There is no pleasant solution" (Dr. Paddock). "The fact that in certain countries people die of hunger is not sufficient reason to provide food assistance" (D. Ellerman, representative of the National Security Council in interdepartmental meetings of the American government). "We are in the position of a family who has a litter of puppies; we have to decide which ones will be drowned" (Clinton P. Anderson, U.S. Secretary of Agriculture in 1946).

This policy of "conservative modernization," which dispossesses the peasant of his land and forces him into poverty, assigns him a precise function: to be a work force that is paid as little as possible. Small-scale agriculture on marginal lands does more than to provide a zone of refuge; it also permits the reproduction of the work force at the cheapest possible price (Chonchol 1982). Under these conditions, it is not surprising that social conflicts multiply. One-quarter of the worldwide deaths resulting from violence between 1820 and 1970 are linked to peasant uprisings or conflicts (Prosterman 1979). In Brazil, the Pastoral Land Commission listed 916 conflicts touching 262,000 families and close to two million people between 1979 and 1981. In the State of Maranhao, a rural association organized to try to resist evictions. "The very day of the first meeting—we were going to discuss what measures to take—Sr. Manaré entered the hamlet with nearly 25 jagundos [hired goons] . . . all armed with rifles, revolvers, knives. They didn't even look at our faces, they simply surrounded the hut, closed all the doors, then opened fire. The women and children were massacred with the men. From that day on we have no longer claimed our rights to the land, but our rights to justice" (Conceiçao 1981).

There is poverty and violence, but also poverty and hunger. Twelve thousand persons, of whom a large proportion are women and children, die every day, not of hunger in the strict sense of the word, but of the consequences of malnutrition. One billion two hundred million ill-fed people (20 percent of the population—the poorest fraction) suffer from a deficiency of 550–750 calories per day. This is even more serious for young children, whose organism then uses up the proteins necessary for body growth to make up for the deficiency.

Two-thirds of the women of the Third World suffer from anemia and malnutrition and these women, like others, bear children. Nutritionists have found that babies lacking calories and necessary proteins during their last weeks in the womb and their first months of life will definitely be weakened mentally, because the cells of the brain "programmed" to multiply during that period are unable to do so due to inadequate nutrition: an irreversible situation that ought to be considered even if large-scale consequences will not be measurable for one or two generations.

Poverty and violence, poverty and hunger, but also, poverty and submission, coexist. The responsibility of women to their children, increased by the break up of both marital and village solidarity, obliges them to accept any kind of work under any sort of conditions. This social and biological responsibility causes women to play an important role in perpetuating the dependence of the underdeveloped countries. The International Labor Office lists them as working mothers, working wives, and working sisters. Profit realized by national and international entreprises is maximized by the notion of "extra income for women," which justifies the injustice of sexual inequality in pay. In fact, in many countries, not only has this "extra" income become absolutely necessary for the survival of the family (it is often necessary to have two or three minimum salaries to attain a level of subsistence), but when a woman is alone—one woman in three is head of a household in countries of the Third World—it is the only source of income. One can see how it has become not only economically profitable, but also politically useful, to have women work in the fields and in the factories—is not their docility their main quality? The risk of their asserting themselves is likely to remain minimal for some time to come.

The implacable logic of apartheid appears as some monstrous foreshadowing of trends which seem to be at work everywhere: black women shut off in reservations live in frightening psychological and material destitution and die in great numbers with their children. Nonetheless, enough of them survive to reproduce a work force that labors in the factories, in the fields, and as servant-slaves in white men's houses. (Don't the men have a right to spend a month on the reservation, just time enough to get their wives pregnant?) One wonders if a slightly liberalized version of this model of society might not spread "just like that," innocently, by the force of circumstances. The barbarism of the world may be measured by the way in which it treats its women.

2

Agricultural Labor: The Business of Women

WOMEN WHO ARE WAGE LABORERS IN AGRICULTURE BELONG TO THE underprivileged social strata of the peasantry, found in greatest numbers in Latin America and in Asia. On both of these continents, large property holdings have existed from time immemorial—the holdings of the superior castes in Asia and the *latifundia,* the great estates in Latin America—and it is here that the poor have been coming to work. Africa, which had a very different system of land tenure, is, nevertheless, also witnessing the passing of land into private hands and the establishment of agro-food firms, although with a significant time lag. Whatever their historical background or their recent history of development, on all three continents the methods for exploiting the women's work are the same.

What kind of work does the female work force do? What are women's working conditions, their salaries, their contribution to the family income?

Women who comprise the largest group do not work on the big plantations. Rather, they belong to the rural families without land, and to the smallest landholders, whose land is insufficient in acreage and often inadequate in quality to assure self-sufficiency in food. The development of a class of women wage earners is, henceforth, a precise index of the increasing pauperization of a social group.

Everywhere the work of women has the same characteristics: time-consuming, repetitive, meticulous tasks, neither enhancing nor appreciated; temporary work; and low pay, lower pay than that received by men for identical work—pay that does not assure survival of a family, pay predominantly by the hour or by the piece. (In India, the proportion of women working at piece rates has gone from 25 percent to 85 percent in sixteen years.) Finally, there is the double workday, since the woman also has to assume her functions as housewife: the drudgery of getting water and wood, preparing the meals, and taking care of children.

21

They hire themselves out as day workers in the fields of medium and large landowners at the time of sowing, planting, weeding, and harvesting, but they also gather the palm nuts in northeastern Brazil. As land has been monopolized by cattle breeders and *grileiros* (land grabbers), women are able to retain only half of the harvest, while the other half is sold to the landowner at a price that he himself fixes. At the beginning of 1980, a nut gatherer found herself rich with 42 centavos to 58 centavos at the end of the day, when at the same time a kilo (2.2 lbs.) of rice cost between 27 centavos and 33 centavos and a kilo of green beans between 42 centavos and 50 centavos (Elgin and Thery 1982). Also, in Minas Gerais, where 66.5 percent of the land is in the hands of a few landowners, women work in the reforestation industry. In all weather and in a bent position for hours, they bed the seedlings for the tree nurseries. They even eat standing up. In Kenya, they husk corn or work on the sugarcane plantations. In Bangladesh, in 50 percent of the families, the paid work of women contributes more than 60 percent to the total income of the family (Agarwal 1981). Women often work in the "Food for Work" programs of the government.

In Brazil, where, according to the census taken by the Institute of Geography and Statistics in 1980, the poorest half of the population has lost one-third of its income in ten years, a majority of women and children, as well as men, wait every day at the roadsides to be picked up by the trucks that take them to work—often for twelve hours—on the coffee, sugar cane, soybean and cocoa plantations (Rullant 1982). In South Africa, 35 percent of the agricultural helpers are women. One could add to the list, but to what purpose?

The poverty and psychological misery of these day workers, caught in a chronic situation of underemployment, contributes to their influx into the cities. There they hope to find a more stable source of income for themselves and their children.

At the same time, a rather large number of rural women sometimes have the possibility of earning a salary on a more regular, though never permanent, basis, either on plantations or in the large agro-business farms. Numerous case studies describe the conditions of their life and show the structural phenomena that account for the specific way in which these working women are exploited.

For example, in Sri Lanka the plantations of tea, rubber, and coconut, anywhere from 24.7–1,235 acres in size, created by the British toward the end of the nineteenth century, have functioned from the beginning with a work force of Tamil Indians—belonging to lower castes or to the Untouchables (Kurian 1980). However, beginning in 1860 the structure of the migration changed, and entire families came and were lodged mostly on the tea plantations. The use of a female work force, paid less than the men, took on an increasing importance: 2.6 percent in 1893, 26.87 percent in 1966, and 51.1 percent in 1977. Independence and the nationalization of these estates did not change the alien character of the work force. The Ceylonese, on the other hand, created family plantations given over mainly to rubber and coconuts, and there they used Ceylonese women of the lower castes. In fact, these women found themselves alone with children to care for, and they were obliged to become wage eagners as a result of the increasing pauperization which impelled the men to emigrate. The women did the unskilled, labor-intensive work: gathering tea leaves, incising the rubber plants and hoeing around the coconut palms.

Let us follow a Tamil tea-picker, housed at the plantation, during one of her work-days. She wakes up at 4:00 A.M. and goes to get the water, for there are no wells near the living quarters. She makes the meal for her husband and children, gets the children ready for school, and eats her own meal. She goes off, leaving the youngest child at the day nursery, if there is one, or with an old woman. Often she must also supply milk for the day. All this has to be finished before she has to make rollcall at 7:00 A.M.—some days at 6:00 A.M. If she is a few minutes late, she will be sent home, thus missing a day's work. But if a woman is pregnant, tardiness is accepted, provided that she makes up the lost time at the end of the day. Then she walks to the field—sometimes several miles away—where she picks the young tea leaves until four, or until five-thirty whenever the harvest is abundant. At noon, there is a break of one hour during which she weighs her morning's harvest, takes care of her youngest child, and eats. The work of picking demands sustained attention, because the slightest mistake, such as choosing tough instead of tender leaves, is punished by dismissal or by a fine. One can see that the discipline is rigorous. The time used for two weighings, one in the middle of the day and the other in the evening, does not count as working time. She returns home, gathers wood on the way, and gets the necessary water for making the evening meal, for washing clothes or for the children's needs. Ceylonese women, who live a certain distance from the plantations, have even less time to get all their chores done. All the women go to sleep between nine and eleven o'clock. This makes for a double workday of fifteen to sixteen hours.

Even though a wage board oversees the salaries of the plantations, for identical work women draw 25 percent less pay than men. The division of labor on the different plantations, which confines women to labor-intensive tasks, is arranged so that women are paid less, while working longer than men. In 1979, on rubber plantations, men worked 16,322 days, receiving a daily wage of 12.72 *roupies*, while women worked 16,591 days for a daily pay of 8.12 *roupies*. In order to make more money, the women try to work longer hours, to do more than the normal work quota, but again they are penalized by the system, because an overtime kilo, according to complicated and peculiar calculations, is paid at a rate 30–40 percent less than a kilo gathered during the "legal" workday. Women workers on the rubber and coconut plantations are subjected to the same unfair system.

The wages, though paid once a month, are not a monthly salary, since they are merely the total of the daily earnings, which depend on the harvest and the season. In fact, they amount to piecework paid on a monthly basis. The average number of workdays is from 16.4–21.9, entailing important variations in the wage earner's income. In short, a family with two people employed on the plantations earns between 225 and 789 *roupies*, the last amount indicating a great deal of overtime. In the tea plantations, the average monthly salary for men is 125 *roupies* and for women, 93.44; they earn 134 and 77.53 *roupies* respectively on the coconut plantations. (These figures are from 1976.)

The salary of the women and other members of the family residing on the plantations of Sri Lanka is almost always handed over to the husband. It is he who takes care of the bills and it seems that women have practically nothing to say about it. Needless to say, there are many quarrels on payday, for example, when the men go out to drink. On the other hand, the women who are nonresidents, whose husbands have gone to find work elsewhere, as well as the women who have been able to choose a husband independently, receive their salaries directly and handle the money themselves.

The only security that women have comes from the system of buying foodstuffs on credit at the village store. On payday they receive their wages, with a deduction made for the purchases of the preceding month, which, however, cannot exceed a certain sum. Money from the wages goes almost exclusively for food, with

10 percent for drink and cigarettes for the men. Other expenses—clothing, shoes, baptisms, marriage—are financed by credit and obtained by pawning some of the possessions of the family or the women.

More than 98 percent of the workers are in debt. The average amount of indebtedness is 400–500 *roupies,* which puts them in a state of complete dependence, especially since the rates of interest are very high. For example, they are forced to buy in the stores run by the lenders, who sell them merchandise at higher prices.

In spite of all these difficulties, these are the relatively lucky women, since they receive a salary every month, even if it is very small and varies somewhat. On the other hand, they have a right to a minimum of social services. The expenses of childbirth are paid by the plantation, which also adds a sum corresponding to forty-two days of work. Some day nurseries, more or less well-run, but insufficient in number, are at their disposal. With so many constraints weighing on these women in their work and at home, they would not be able to continue to help support their family without their daughters' assistance. The latter, therefore, play a major role in perpetuating these miserable working conditions. This underlying aspect emerges each time that poverty and destitution submerge the family. Not surprisingly the schooling of the girls suffers: on the plantations a drop in the level of instruction among young women coincides with an increase in economic difficulties.

If the state-owned plantations assure women a minimum of regularity in their poverty, it is not the same in the agro-business sector. The latter, developing especially in Latin America, but also in Africa, puts into practice a more inexorable international system of exploiting women workers: uncertain and irregular salary, piece work, intensive and physically exhausting labor, no social benefits, and inequality of remuneration as between men and women, amplified by a sexual division of labor that reserves those tasks that get the highest remuneration to men.

Near Dakar, the Bud Company, created with American and Dutch capital in 1972, became in 1974 a mixed company in which the Senegalese have a majority interest (Kane 1977). Established on lands given by the state in accordance with the law on the National Domain, Bud raises off-season vegetables, such as tomatoes, green peppers, eggplant, melons, green beans, and some fruit, such as strawberries and mangoes. It employs a seasonal work force—six months of the year—made up mainly of women, for men cannot stand stoop labor. Women are therefore employed in harvesting, while the men, in smaller numbers, are given mechanized tasks, such as packaging.

Exporting eight thousand tons of produce in 1973, Bud employed 176 year-round people and between fourteen and sixteen hundred seasonal workers. Hours of work varied according to the season and the productivity of the fields: eight and a half hours a day, seven days a week in the slack season, twelve hours a day, seven days a week at the height of the season. Two hours walking time to get to the fields should be added to this schedule.

For the same task the hourly remunerations were unequal: 40 CFA Fr. [French African Community Francs] was paid to women and 50 CFA Fr. to men who were packers. For other tasks the wage per hour varied, according to classification, between 54.85 and 120 CFA Fr. No woman earned more than 59.91 CFA Fr. per hour. Monthly salaries ranged between 5,000 and 10,000 CFA Fr. [Early in 1987 the going rate was 324 CFA Fr. = one U.S. dollar.]

These low salaries made it necessary for the women—the wives of small peasants of the area—to continue with their previous activities: the growing and marketing of vegetables produced on their own plots of land and the selling of vegetables grown on their husband's land. This double employment required organizing all the women into extended families, taking in everyone from little girls to grandmothers.

In the State of Sinaloa, in northeastern Mexico, the government has encouraged concentration of land into fewer hands and penetration by foreign capital (such as the Mexican Colorado Rises Land Co., Kansas Sinaloa Investment Co., and Sinaloa Irrigation Co.). The State of Sinaloa, which comprises only 3 percent of all land in Mexico, includes, on the other hand, 18 percent of all the irrigated lands on which tomato and vegetable growers have established themselves since the twenties (Roldan 1981). In 1975, foreign trade in these crops amounted to ten thousand million pesos, corresponding to one million fifty eight thousand tons of fresh vegetables (tomatoes, cucumbers, and onions) which represent 36 percent of the agricultural export of the entire country.

There are no precise statistics on the number of workers employed on these agro-farms. According to Maulio Tirardo, in 1978–79 there were one hundred sixty thousand seasonal laborers in for the harvest and the packaging of vegetables and sugar cane, among whom one hundred thousand were young girls (Roldan 1981). About 50 percent of the field hands are women and about 90 percent of them are in packaging. In large part, this work force comes from the poor, nonirrigated zones where the low productivity of subsistence farming of corn and sorghum forces men and women to emigrate in search of temporary work to augment their income in order to get through the year.

The Garcia enterprise is given over to the growing of tomatoes. The sexual division there is strict: women select and pack the tomatoes; men do all the other jobs, such as transporting, labeling, and sealing; in the fields, women sow, while men prepare the soil, put in the stakes and spread the fertilizer.

The pay is the same for men and women for the same jobs— 19.70 pesos per hour and 158 pesos per day for harvesting and packing. Yet the men are employed mainly at the more skilled jobs, resulting in considerable pay differences: five thousand pesos per week for men, and twelve hundred pesos a week for women.

The erratic aspect of the work hinges on prices in the American market and sometimes on weather conditions. It is rare that a woman can work an entire week. During the year, work on these agro-farms lasts about six months for most of the women, from the second half of December until the first week of June, which corresponds to the season when Florida cannot supply the American market, since this is the season of frost.

The women work from 7:30 A.M.–12:30 P.M. and then from 1:30–4:30 P.M. for harvesting, but from 8:30 A.M. until noon only for the packaging, which permits young mothers to take care of their children in the afternoons. The men refuse to work on the packing assembly, where any break for taking a drink or smoking a cigarette is forbidden. The packaging also depends on the quantity of tomatoes harvested, and the line may be stopped for lack of ripe tomatoes or for lack of electricity or packing supplies.

The salary of the young unmarried women represents up to one-fifth of the family income. Seventy-five percent of this salary, handled by the mother, goes for food, 10 percent for shoes and clothing, 8 percent for school expenses, and the remainder for medicine. The married women, or those living with someone, having six or eight children, as well as the women who are heads of household, bring in between 80 percent and 70 percent of the family income, but cannot make do without the help of their daughters. Yet the pay is insufficient and the women have to try to earn more by doing laundry, ironing, housework, or preparing meals and drinks for sale.

In the region of Sabana, near Bogota, Colombia, land

ownership is highly concentrated, since about 2 percent of the landowners control more than 50 percent of the land; the owners having less than about seven and a half acres cannot survive on the income from their crops (Silva de Rojas 1981). In all these families it has become vital that at least two or three members hire themselves out. They continue, nevertheless, to work their own land, but this is after a workday elsewhere and on their days off.

The great estates either raise cattle (10 percent of the gross national product of Colombia—the third greatest Latin-American milk producer after Brazil and Argentina) or flowers. Thanks to the support of the government by way of the Export Promotion Fund, the flower-growing sector (roses, mums and carnations) has undergone enormous expansion for about a dozen years. In 1968, there were about 15 acres and a production of 150 tons; in 1978, there were 85 plantations and 26,083 tons. The exports, which amount to about $800,000,000, are directed mainly to the U.S. (74.3 percent) and Europe. Women are used, for the most part, for this unskilled manual labor. The hiring policy is twofold: an enterprise like Rosas Lindas hires young unmarried girls without children; another, Florandia, hires women whose childbearing days are almost over. In each case, maternity payments are avoided. Young mothers kept out of certain jobs by these practices have to look for other work, which they sometimes find on dairy farms. They do the milking from 5:00–7:00 A.M. and from 3:00–5:00 P.M., hours that allow them to take care of their children, though the work pays badly (Silva de Rojas 1981).

Again in Mexico, where between 1964–74 food production per inhabitant decreased by 10 percent in ten years, production for export increased by 27 percent. The United States has invested more in Mexico than in any other country (Burbach and Flynn 1978). In this way, the valley of Zamora has become a large producer of strawberries. Situated 350 kilometers northeast of Mexico City, this valley, where the haciendas had been dismantled by the land reform under Cardenas during the '30s, experienced again in the 1950s the concentration of land ownership. Aided by Americans, the former proprietors, having switched to commerce and banking, financed the development of traditional farming, but especially of new crops such as strawberries (Arizpe and Aranda 1981). In 1968 there were 4,250 acres of strawberries; in 1970, there were 8,140 acres; in 1973, there were 8,615; and in 1980, there were 6,062 acres. This most recent drop came after a crisis in 1971 due to overproduction and a slump in strawberries owing to competition from California. To avoid similar misadventures, the government limited production acreage by having the secretary of agriculture and irrigation deliver all authorizations for this use of the land. These were monopolized by the large private landowners, assigned about 88 percent of the authorized acreage, with the rest going to village communities and small individual farmers. The total represents about 12,350 acres of strawberries.

This great increase was accompanied by an influx of migrant workers, 50,000 in all, mostly women who came in search of work in this region. The agro-strawberry business employs 11,110 permanent salaried workers, of whom 5,068 women are in the freezing sector and in packaging, and 27,775 seasonal workers, of whom 16,875 are women employed for about three months.

The workers are young, 78.6 percent from fifteen to twenty-four years of age, but 10 percent are younger still, between twelve and fifteen years of age. During the peak periods, the enterprise recruits women of all ages. Workers over thirty are usually divorcees, women who have been deserted, or widows having complete charge of their families. It is obvious that the average salary—varying between 750 and 1,750 pesos per month—is clearly below the legal minimum wage set at 4,260 pesos per month and in no way permits a family to make a living.

To force women to work at such low wages that they have to find extra work if they want to assume their first responsibility—to perpetuate the labor force—accentuates their economic dependence and their docility. At the same time, the social and economic superiority of men (however illusory), for whom the most skilled jobs are reserved, yet who are themselves inadequately paid, reinforces the women's sense of inferiority. They can do stoop labor, and the men cannot. In this terrible con game, all the poor lose.

3

The Cocoa Bean Divides the Family

IN AFRICA, UNLIKE ASIA AND LATIN AMERICA, THE SYSTEM OF LAND distribution has retained a collectivist character, while the development of production for export has been and continues to be carried out mainly within the framework of family farming. Through the effect of a historical lag, this continent is still at the stage where one may observe the transition from an agricultural society where the sexes complement each other to a modern society where they clash and compete with each other.

This major movement starts from a relative equilibrium which is still uneven, where the men make war, hunt, fish, and take part in politics, but also do the clearing and spade work in the fields, while the women's planting and gathering assures the feeding of the family. The proportion in which men and women participate in farming is obviously not uniform throughout the continent; it varies according to the country and the society. There is a complementarity in fact and law—a respect for the contribution of each—which shows up in a very strict division of duties and obligations. In most countries, putting men to work in agriculture coincided with colonization, with the development of export crops and the rise of a money economy.

It is at this point that social disruption begins: men, though continuing to rely on women's traditional assistance, claim the entire income from the cash-producing export crops for themselves. Money, because of its very newness, need not be divided in traditional ways. It has a way of renewing male power, which now becomes crassly economic, instead of being masked by traditional religious beliefs. As for women, they keep their old domain, that of family food growing; but family food growing, deprived of all monetary prestige, becomes the negative pole of the family economy. Nevertheless, since they retain the same tasks, women are faced with a fundamental contradiction; they need money to carry out their obligations, but they are relegated to an unproductive sphere monetarily, by the men of their family, by the state, and by

30

those responsible for development. It is when the scale of social and economic value tilts that an irreversible change makes women aware of their condition. It is only then that they make demands; refuse, confront, and with surprising inventiveness do battle in a thousand and one ways, in order to break out of an economic sterility to which they are being condemned.

It remains nonetheless true that women in Africa still perform 70 percent even 80 percent of the agricultural work, 50 percent of the cattle raising, and about 100 percent of the conversion of agricultural raw materials. In doing this they assure a major part in the feeding of the continent (Food and Agricultural Organization 1979). Yet it is also true that women, barred from agricultural extension programs and from credit systems and cooperatives— the only access to innovation—are unable to increase their productivity as farmers (Loufti 1980).

Under these conditions, what is the sense of the countless discussions on food self-sufficiency from which women are barred? What is the basis for this blind unwillingness, or perhaps inability, to consider women as the economic partners of men? In the Congo, 68.49 percent of the cultivated land belongs to the peasant sector, which in this particular country is almost exclusively in the hands of women—men having only recently been involved in commercial farming (Bisilliat 1982). It is one example, among many others: improbable as it may seem, none of the development projects intended to increase food production for family consumption directly address women. Were it not for the fact that such aberrations help account for hunger in Africa, this might seem a laughing matter.

To understand the economic problems of women in Africa, it is essential to grasp their traditional relationship to the land and to time. In Africa, women have always had the *usufruct* (right of usage) of plots of land that their husbands grant them for growing vegetables, plants used for seasonings, and basic family food crops. But the practice of growing crops for cash income, reserved for the men, is progressively taking up the best lands and encroaching on the space previously allotted for producing basic food crops. The fields, farther and farther from the village, have soil of varying quality. The decrease in the area cultivated for family food crops tends to cut down the length of time the land is permitted to lie fallow, further impoverishing the soil and bringing about a continuous drop in yields.

When the lands are redistributed, the traditional landed status of women contributes to excluding them from the new method of land distribution. For example, in 1979, the Société d'aménagement et d'exploitation du delta, the public authority charged with the development of the central valley of Senegal, organized a drawing of lots among farm heads in order that everyone, independent of their social standing (for example, former slaves, craftsmen, and "lords"), would have an equal chance in the distribution of farming parcels in the village's irrigated area. But this sense of justice has its limits. Whatever their status—wives, single women, or actual heads of households—women were essentially barred from this land distribution. It became necessary for the neediest, such as one widow with four children, to get around the difficulty, by furnishing, with the consent of the villagers, a fictitious head of household: a five-year-old son or a dead relative (Fiéloux 1980).

Under the pressure of commercial farming, women's time spent on farm work has increased and now exceeds that of men. In Central Africa, they work from 28–33 percent longer (Agarval 1981). In the Congo, women work two hundred days per year and men, thirty. In Gambia, the women devote twenty hours per week to the work on the land; the men, nine (Palmer 1977).

Type of Work	Percentage of Total Work Time in Hours	
	Men	Women
Cutting down of trees and preparing fields	95	5
Plowing	70	30
Seeding and planting	50	50
Weeding	30	70
Harvesting	40	60
Bringing in harvest	20	80
Stockpiling harvest	20	80
Transforming food products	10	90
Taking food products to market and selling them	40	60
Pruning trees	90	10
Getting water and fuel	10	90
Taking care of domestic animals and cleaning stables	50	50
Hunting	90	10
Feeding and caring for children, men, elderly	5	95

Besides, women's work, consuming as it does much time and energy, does not stop when the fieldwork is done. Women face such irksome tasks as getting water and wood, which often means transporting heavy loads over several miles; they transform products in preparation for meals, such as crushing millet, hulling and picking rice, or grinding tapioca, work of about three or four hours a day for a medium-sized family. Moreover, a balanced diet—mainly vitamins and lipids—depends as well on what the economists laughably call "non-productive" time that the women invest in gathering caterpillars, larvae, leaves, and roots, and transforming products into oils and vegetable butters. Finally, insofar as they are the ones mainly responsible for small trading, the women sell or exchange the agricultural surplus in its crude or processed form and in return obtain food products not produced at home, such as salt, spices, and meat. In short, these overworked women, borne down by the hundreds of tasks demanded of them and who put in fourteen–nineteen-hour days, largely assure the survival of the family labor force. They are hardly underemployed as one is often expected to believe (Boserup 1970).

In order to provide a historical perspective on the way the introduction of export crops alters a social group and affects women's role in the economy, we have chosen one specific instance. Our case in point deals with the Adioukrou palm groves on the Ivory Coast between 1920–80 (Dupire and Boutillier 1958; Traoré 1981). This example outlines the progressive and continuous changes in the organization of tasks and the distribution of income between men and women. We will cite the specific problems of the Adioukrou women, with emphasis on those that concern rural women in general, regardless of the village community to which they belong.

It is possible to distinguish three main periods in the evolution of the Adioukrou mode of production. During the first period, which extended from 1920–50, the Adioukrou cultivated natural palm groves. Beneath the palms and in separate parcels of land, they grew produce for home consumption such as cassava, plantain, and vegetables. Since 1925–30, at the urging of the colonial administration, they also produced coffee and cocoa for export. At this time the division of labor between men and women was rather well-defined, as was the sharing of income; the women had a certain economic independence, thanks to their agricultural labor and their trading. "The household is but a linking of two lineages, which join forces in the common expenditures for subsistence, but which retain a strong autonomy in the use of their income" (Traoré 1981). Such association is known almost everywhere in Africa.

Except for the felling of trees, stump removal, and plowing, which are always done by men, the production of food for the family is the work of women. In addition, women are responsible for the harvest, and for transporting and transforming the products grown. For example, they devote two days a week to the preparation of tapioca flour, a staple food.

In the palm plantations, the men do the spadework, clear and cut the clusters. Women of all ages take part in the other operations: the youngest carry the clusters to the encampment, a very difficult job "because it is necessary to cover several hundred meters with an ill balanced, heavy load of 110 pounds on one's head" (Traoré 1981). The oldest women gather the scattered grains. The collaboration of women is equally indispensable in the village: it is the women who remove the pulp, who help in the making of the oil (the first boiling), and grind the nuts. The men also have certain jobs, but the time that they devote to this is "appreciably less than that of the women" (Traoré 1981). Nevertheless, there is a sharing of income between men and women. The latter receive oil in kind from the second boiling and some palm cabbages or an equivalent in money, about 38 percent of the revenue of the palm grove.

This social and economic system recognizes and values men's and women's tasks as complementary. But the development of production for export leads to another way of dividing the revenue: men keep the income from the cultivation of coffee and cocoa, demanding at the same time that the women help them in the traditional way with the harvest, the carrying, and the crushing. Women receive only a symbolic compensation for their work: two pieces of cloth each year and the right to glean, that is, to gather whatever beans may be left after the regular harvest. It is in this way that "the cocoa bean divides the family and destroys kinship."

This situation is not peculiar to the Adioukrou. It exists everywhere in rural areas where commercial growing takes root. The effects of the development of commercial farming on women often show up in identical ways. First of all, commercial farming leads to an increase in the working time of the women farm workers, while bringing about an increasing differentiation in productivity between men and women. "When modernization entails some particularly painstaking operations and others that are highly productive, the former are customarily given to women" (Palmer 1977). On the other hand, the tasks that are labor-intensive are accomplished, even in a rural development project, with traditional tools. The sexual division of work corresponds, in fact, to an unequal allocation of the means of production. The mechanized work, the plowing and clearing, is always done by men; it is the same for most of the activities tied to new farming techniques—fertilizers, insecticides, or irrigation. On the contrary, the women do work that requires traditional know-how, but they also do work such as bedding out the rice among the Toucouleur, work that the men quickly deem too time-consuming and which they claim is "easy for women and children."

However, the participation of the women in production for the market allows a lowering of the cost of production by avoiding exclusive reliance on paid workers. This "subsidy" is especially interesting, since women workers get but a miniscule part of the revenues in the guise of different kinds of gifts. For example, a Diola woman (in Senegal) who works in the peanut fields of her husband, receives a basket of peanuts in the shell, the value of which is between 1,000 and 2,000 CFA Fr. for her work, that is, about one-twentieth of the income that her husband realizes from the sale of the harvest (Journet 1981).

But those women used to their old independent economic status do not always easily accept these new working conditions, which turn them into an unpaid labor force. Occasionally revolts break out: the Bamileke women (in Cameroon) destroyed a number of coffee plantations between 1956–62; the Gbeye women (in Central Africa) launched a general strike in order to oppose the use of family mutual aid (formerly used only in subsistence farming) in the cotton fields, as cotton was an export product (Gosselin 1978). One may further cite the almost universal sporadic strikes against the midday meals that have to be carried to the men in the fields.

Conflict about work can even lead to divorce. In the region of Bete of the Ivory Coast, where the plantation economy started to develop around 1925–30, the situation forty years later is described in this way: "The conjugal relationship has a tendency to become increasingly like that of employer and employee, in spite of the family structure's appearance of neutrality: the male proprietor of the land uses his wife as labor. In this capacity he is required to pay her compensation in cash, established on the basis of the harvest of coffee and of cocoa. Such a situation brings about conflicts when a man no longer pays his wife or pays her

poorly and she has a right to challenge the marriage contract"
(Dozon 1977). Matrimonial instability, which has greatly increased, demonstrates that this clause is not respected. The men
of Bete prefer to give several loincloths at harvest time, rather
than money. In 1974, at a meeting in Bete, the women again
demanded to be paid at least like laborers. "We are not animals,"
they said. "We would like to be paid for our work."

During the second period, between 1950–60, one witnessed
among the Adioukrou the stifling of women's handicrafts. It was
in 1960 that "the first large technical revolution occurred." It
concerned the installation, in the city of Dabou, of a modern oil
processing plant designed to extract oil from the palm clusters
collected by the plant's trucks. In fact, this mill was a resounding
failure during its first years, because the supplies of clusters
amounted to one-fourth of the anticipated 40,000 tons per year, a
figure already well below the theoretical production capacity of
the palm plantation. This failure was of such a magnitude that the
technical and social causes had to be examined.

One of the main impediments seems to have stemmed from
conflicts between men and women of the same lineage. As a
matter of fact, the elimination of the manual extraction of oil and
the delivery of the clusters to the factory introduced a serious
imbalance between men and women as far as work and the allot-
ment of income was concerned. From the new system "the men
obtained all of the advantages," since it provided them with more
leisure time, while permitting them to retain nearly all of the
income. As for the women, if they saved time, they lost their main
source of income. In addition, their pay for the only work still left
to them—carrying the clusters over a longer distance to the collection points—"is left for the men to decide. The latter, while
recognizing the wrong done to the women, did not believe it was
necessary to right the wrong by instituting appropriate remuneration" (Dupire and Bouthillier 1958; Traoré 1981). Under the impact of the changes in the process of production, of which the
oilmill at Dabou is but one example, a double movement of economic and social decline began and intensified: income for
women dwindled year after year and the women peasants were
relegated to subsistence farming, which became deprived of prestige and thought of as merely "good" for feeding the family. Yet
the women's obligation to take sole and exclusive charge of family
food production led to a certain number of difficulties.

One notes, first, a lessening of the quantity and diversity of the
crops grown because of the lack of time, labor, tools, and fertile

land. Thus in Kenya, the Kikuyu women have lost certain parcels of land that they could have used, such as the bottom land where they grew rice and sweet potatoes. Furthermore, they are obliged to buy, at their own expense, the necessary fertilizer for the poor soil of the fields which they are allotted (Stamp 1975). On the other hand, since the men have abandoned the rice fields to concentrate on commercial peanut growing, the Diola women from Senegal have not been able to use the traditional tools utilized by the men. They have replaced these with a long-handled hoe, which allows them to work faster and more easily, but which only scratches the surface of the soil, thereby permitting many more weeds to grow. This practice results in much weeding under very difficult conditions during the rainy season, and, finally, in a great drop in productivity and income (Journet 1981).

In addition, one staple product is sometimes substituted for another of lesser nutritional value, simply because the latter is easier to grow. For example, before the introduction of cocoa plantations in Ghana, the men were in charge of planting and harvesting yams, while women took part in the harrowing. The yams produced went to the men and their families. On their own plots of land, the women grew corn and some vegetables. When the men devoted themselves to growing cocoa, they left the growing of yams to women, but pocketed the income from that harvest. With their only income, the women then had to take over the buying of such customary items as fish, salt, and meat, as well as articles for the household. This abusive upholding of a former right, the lengthy labor demanded by the yam (because of the mounding and staking), the lack of workers, and the need to work in the cocoa fields, forced women to replace the yam with the cassava, a secondary cultivation until then (Buck 1976).

This social devaluing of subsistence farming was aggravated by the absence of a price policy at the governmental level, at the very time when commercial farmers were partly subsidized by the authorities. Several consequences follow from this state of affairs: on one hand, the daily remuneration of a worker on a cocoa farm (330 CFA Fr.) is considerably higher than that for a worker on a family farm producing food for the home (130 CFA Fr.) (Bessat and Trouvé 1982). On the other hand, women are not able to clear any surplus for investment from their long and difficult labor on the subsistence plots.

Whether it be in Africa, Latin America, or Asia, in rural zones the introduction of new technologies in agriculture always produces imbalances comparable to those just described. In brief, new technologies—an oil press, a husking mill, a dairy—contribute to creating underemployment and unemployment in the female work force, thereby impoverishing women. It has been calculated that the introduction of small huskers in Javanese villages has caused women to lose twelve million days of work per year. This represents a lost income of $55 million, the equivalent of more than four months of full-time work for one million women (Collier 1975).

Finally, during the period from 1960–80, in the country of the Adioukrou farming for export became diversified, and the displacement of the women intensified. The policy of agricultural diversification, advocated after independence, led to the "palm plan" being put into effect by SODEPALM (the Society for the Development and Cultivation of the Oil-producing Palm). Yields increased due to the use of new production techniques put into effect in the industrial plantations. But they sanctioned more categorically than ever, the exclusion of women from the modern economic sector. The men, the only economic partners recognized by SODEPALM, became the proprietors of the plantations, from which they have drawn a good revenue given the stability of world prices for palm oil. Ousted from this area, women no longer have the right to grow cassava beneath the palms as before. They are now obliged to grow it on whatever land is left over from the growing of export crops. Furthermore, their situation is complicated in that the men, busy with their export crops, often refuse to do the cutting and clearing of a new plot when it is intended merely for the women (Dupire and Bouthillier 1958; Traoré 1981).

In adapting themselves to these new economic conditions, women have found another activity to bring in money: the making and marketing of tapioca flour, *attieke*, of which Abidjan (the capital city) consumes a great deal (fifty tons a day in 1980, of which 70 percent comes from this region). The women therefore have to grow as much manioc as possible. In view of the men's lack of cooperation, they have few options open to them. They could employ workers to clear their plot of land (but the operation is costly), or they can cultivate a family plot and buy from the holder of this plot, a husband or an uncle, a portion of the harvest at a price slightly below the market price. This involves time-consuming, monotonous labor and is poorly paid (Traoré 1981).

The general balance sheet is very negative: in about thirty years, the situation of the Adioukrou women, like that of other women producers, has deteriorated considerably. From the original, unequal situation where men at least respected the status and role of women has evolved a situation of still greater inequity, whereby their control of the economy has given men a chance to monopolize the advantages and profits brought about by the modernization of agriculture.

In the meantime, women are faced with the same economic obligations as before, but they have progressively been deprived of the sources of income needed to meet them. Edged out, they are treated like creatures apart and deprived of the rights that would allow them access to new income. Rather than teaching them the new techniques of farming and management which they are perfectly capable of mastering, preference is given to teaching them embroidery, sewing, knitting, and cooking. Surely, the height of folly is to teach young women in a Congolese village to please their children by frying fritters made of wheat flour— nowhere to be found in the bush—at a time when these same women do not earn enough money to buy a bit of fish or meat.

Women are also deprived of access to credit. They are not considered solvent enough, or sufficiently responsible, to qualify for loans. On the rare occasions when they are allowed a loan, the result is completely paradoxical: the rate of repayment imposed on women is slightly higher than that for men (Upper Volta). Yet the risks incurred by the lending institutions are no higher than with men; studies have shown that women are good risks (Stamp 1975).

They are, moreover, excluded from existing cooperatives. For example, the Kikuyo women (in Kenya) managed to grow coffee on their own, but were not permitted to avail themselves of the (sales) cooperatives, institutions that are exclusively male and of which, moreover, their own husbands are members. The husbands paid back only a small part of the profits to their wives,

Access According to Sex to Training
Programs in Africa (Percentages)

(Economic and Social Council/Food and Agricultural
Organization 1974)

	MEN	WOMEN
Agriculture	85	15
Cattle raising on small scale	80	20
Cooperatives	90	10
Handicrafts	50	50
Nutrition	10	90
Family economy	0	100

keeping the greater part for themselves to be spent on personal expenditures, such as drink. Seeing this money from the sale of their coffee get away from them, the women had but one choice left: ironically and bitterly baptizing it "booze coffee," they gave it up as a crop. As women are discouraged from joining existing co-ops, they are also denied assistance in organizing producers and marketing cooperatives of their own.

In the face of this social rejection, this harsh and stressful life, even more, these economic obstacles in the form of new taboos, it is not surprising that women should be increasingly tempted to leave for the big cities in the often deceptive hope of finding work there.

4

The Migrations

FOR TWO DECADES, MILLIONS OF WOMEN HAVE BEEN FORCED TO leave their villages, as their economic situation and that of their families has deteriorated. This phenomenon, which has reached its greatest scope in Latin America, corresponds to the decline in women's participation in the agricultural sector. Fifty-eight percent of women moving to Santiago, Chile, were unemployed or looking for work in the rural areas from which they came, compared to 21 percent of the men (Elizaga 1970). In Lima, during the period of 1956–65, these figures were 74 percent and 45 percent respectively (Peru, Direccion National de Estadisticas y Censos 1955–1969). Even though men predominate in migrations from one rural area to another, nowadays more women than men are leaving for the cities: there are eighty-five men to every one hundred women. In Latin America from 1969–79, approximately 3.8 million women swelled the urban proletariat (Arizpe 1981). In Asia this phenomenon does not have exactly the same characteristics. Migrations there involved, above all, single men or else men accompanied by their families; nonetheless, the proportion of women migrants has begun to increase in certain countries (United Nations 1980). In the Philippines in 1961, 62 percent of the migrants were women, and 69 percent of them were between eleven and twenty years of age. By contrast, in northern India, women are not allowed to migrate: only 7 percent of the migrants were women (Connell and Dasgupta 1976). In northern and northeastern Thailand, where the population lives below the poverty threshold, the exodus of women is part and parcel of many a family's strategy for survival.

Africa is beginning to follow this same migratory process. Until recently in rural areas the rate of illiteracy among women often still approached 90 percent. The propensity to emigrate on the part of girls seems to be a corollary of the development of schooling. This also holds true for Cameroon, where more than 60 percent of the boys and girls are enrolled in school and in the

Diola region of Senegal as well (Bessat and Trouvé 1982). Yet neither in Asia nor in Africa have the migrations changed the sex ratio of the urban population, as is the case in Latin America, where there are ninety men to every one hundred women (Arizpe 1981).

In general, women migrants are either young girls, who at about the age of fifteen leave to help support their families, or else they are women heading households, who emigrate for lack of land or lack of work. The departure of girls does not have quite the same significance as that of boys. Female emigration results chiefly from the deterioration of employment and pay for women. In Latin America, a correlation has been established between the decreasing age of female migrants and increasing poverty of the family; girls, therefore, are called upon to go make money in the cities by the time they are ten–twelve years old. It is the same in the Philippines. Girls without any immediate or fore-seeable prospect of paid work cannot be expected to remain at home, particularly when they are no longer needed to work the tiny plots of available land. Besides, changes in the marriage customs may tend in the same direction: in Mexico, marriageable daughters no longer even bring to their family the free labor of the sons-in-laws, as the latter have abandoned the ancient custom of living with their in-laws for the first several years. This change has reinforced the more immediate economic factors that stimu-late the feminine exodus (Young 1978). Young girls leave in order to better help their family: working in the city means being able to send money, medicine and clothes back home.

With this in mind, people in the Philippines prefer to send a daughter rather than a son to the city, knowing that she will be more conscious of her responsibilities and that she will not waste money on her own personal needs. In Senegal, daughters do not hesitate to quit school to hire themselves out as servants in Zinguinchor, Kaolak, and especially in Dakar. This exodus is taking place at an increasingly young age and is becoming more and more permanent, to the point where, in some villages, the young men, for whom this poses a marriage problem, are trying to force the young girls to return for the winter season by threat-ening to "tax" them. "The parents find themselves in a contradic-tory economic position: to accept the absence of their daughters is to give up a worker, but also, for the moment, to have one less mouth to feed and possibly to benefit financially as well" (Journet 1981).

In their search for work, women migrate mostly to large cities within their own countries. Only rarely do they emigrate to foreign countries. Taking into account their low level of education—the majority are illiterate and the rest have not finished grade school—these women, whether they are in Lagos, São Paulo, or Bangkok, perform unskilled jobs left unfilled by the city-dwellers, whose educational level is always higher than that of the rural people. In other words, they do the jobs identified as women's work: they are servants in Latin America and in the Philippines, prostitutes in Bangkok, factory workers in Asia, or peddlers in Africa. The proportion of employed women is high among the migrants, for coming as they do from the most poverty-stricken rural areas, they are ready to accept any sort of work under any kind of conditions (Jelin 1977).

The exodus of women is a major social phenomenon because of what it reveals about the disintegration of the family and the material and psychological conditions of life in a metropolitan environment. Since the causes of female migration are structurally tied to the growing pauperization of the countryside, one must expect that the number of women becoming proletarians will increase. A story about Guatemalan peasants demonstrates this reality: the policies of one of the large American food multinationals, Hanover Brands, resulted in women becoming heavily indebted. "They urged us to grow cauliflower and now we no longer have anything to eat." In fact, during the entire harvest period of 1980, women were unable to make any purchases whatever: "Our children were forced to leave home in search of work as farm hands or servants" (Kinley 1982).

Yet rural women may also find themselves in the situation of being the wives, mothers, or daughters of male migrants. Until the last forty years, the earlier phenomenon of male migration predominated. Overpopulation, lack of access to the land on the part of younger sons, indebtedness linked to growing commercial crops, the need for cash—all these socioeconomic reasons drove able-bodied men between twenty–forty years of age to emigrate. Forty–fifty percent of the men of this age group have left the countryside in Cameroon, 30–50 percent in the Mossi region of the Upper Volta, as many in the middle valley of Senegal, and more than two-thirds of the men in Lesotho. Equally high rates of migration have been found in several Asian countries (Thailand, India, Bangladesh, Malaysia) and in Latin America.

Recent studies are beginning to describe the effects of male emigration on the life of the women who remain in the village community, who become, in fact if not by right, heads of households: in Kenya, 36 percent of the families have women heading the household, in the Philippines 20 percent, and in Lesotho, 25 percent (Buvinic and Youssef 1978). However, such women are not necessarily left to their own devices, for in the absence of their husband, a close relative of his, a father or brother, may be asked to replace him and to intervene in decisions concerning farm work, home repairs, the children's education and, more generally, the use to which the money sent by the migrant is put.

In rural areas the disproportion between the number of working men and women caused by migration (1.9 women to every one man in Cameroon and in Senegal) calls for a change in the way a family copes with its traditional tasks. A long-term migration that does not take the agricultural cycle into consideration consequently intensifies women's work: the rate of feminine participation increases (in India, from 43.4–46.6 percent), as does the duration of agricultural work (more than ten hours per day during the growing season in Lesotho and in Malawi). This in turn accentuates trends we have already noted, namely the fact of women increasingly assuming sole charge of family farming, while at the same time having to devote more time to commercial crops. Yet these added responsibilities have gained them neither new appreciation, nor any increase in their rights.

Seasonal migration is a special case that does not entail overwork for women, because the men return to the village at the time of planting. Overwork can also be avoided when the migration is organized in such a way that one or two able-bodied men always remain in the village, the migrants taking turns in leaving (Amselle 1976). The solution of hiring replacement workers is little used, because of most peasants' poverty. Even so, in those Asian countries where the social and economic status of the family is judged by their ability to keep their women in seclusion, hiring someone is a very difficult, though tempting, solution. In real life, the income slated to pay for a replacement worker is used, first, to pay off debts, to buy foodstuffs, or to repair the house (Shaheed 1981).

It is difficult to draw any general conclusion as to the percentage of migrants who send back remittances, or the amounts involved, which seem to vary from one country to another and from one family to the next. Some surveys have been conducted in a number of African countries. By contrast, this type of research has made little headway in Latin America and Asia (International Labour Office 1982).

In Africa, it appears that the migrants' remittances often represent an important part of a family's annual income. For example, in Nigeria, 60 percent of the urban migrants regularly send money back home, which amounts to 20–35 percent of their families' income; in Ghana, between two-fifths and two-thirds of the families have migrant funds at their disposal; in Senegal, 30–50 percent of family income is attributable to the migrants. Yet the funds from migratory workers received by African women far from correspond to these percentages. In fact, considering the increasing number of divorces or threats of divorce for non-support and the wives' constant search for paid work, it would appear that the income they receive in no way meets their needs. What is more, they do not receive these remittances in their own name: one of the close relatives of the migrant worker is normally in charge of doling out the money to the woman. Is this a way of controlling their spending? A woman from Punjab explains: "It is nice that my husband earns a lot of money. I am happy about it, even if he is away. But if I need money, I have to go to my brother-in-law. He gives me some when it doesn't amount to much, but he often tells me that he has to write to my husband to inform him of my request. How do I know what he writes, since I cannot read? How can my husband know what I need, when he is so far away?" (Shaheed 1981).

The wives' presence in the village community may be essential for the kinship group to survive, for migrants leaving with their wives and children practically stop sending money to their village. That is why the elders of a kinship group, using a variety of pretexts, try to prevent the wives' departure, knowing how closely linked that departure is to a major loss of their income. Yet in spite of everything, women who join their migrant husbands are becoming more and more numerous. Much like the single women migrants, almost as great a proportion of these wives will gravitate toward the casual work sector in the cities.

5

Urban Casual Work: Life Must Go On

THESE TIDES OF MEN AND WOMEN MIGRANTS ARE RESPONSIBLE FOR an increase in the rate of urban growth from 4–6 percent each year, twice that of Europe. The 27 percent of the population of the Third World who lived in urban zones in 1975 will number 41 percent in the year 2000. The corollary of this uncontrolled urbanization is the spread of shantytowns—with their trail of poverty and suffering—where more than 60 percent of the city dwellers in Latin America, and nine out of ten of the inhabitants of Calcutta, live.

However, the process of development which caused millions of women to leave their rural areas has not succeeded in completely absorbing this new work force. Full employment in the capitalist economies is a theorist's dream. It would, in fact, be necessary that "the new arrivals on the labor market be fitted into the modern sector, that wage employment absorbed one-half of the working population, whereas in many of the underdeveloped countries the percentage is from 10 to 20 percent." Even "countries where economic growth is relatively rapid experience a drop in salaried employment in terms of the percentage of the active population" (Hugon 1982), together with an increase in underemployment and unemployment.

What work can these women migrants, so poorly educated and almost always unskilled, find in the cities? Some of the youngest will be absorbed by the industrial sector—where it exists—and those who remain, of all ages, will have no other choice, but to rejoin older city women in what is called the casual work or nonstructured sector.

By definition, the activities lumped together in this sector are heterogenous, ranging from water carrier and pack-peddler to heads of family enterprises employing less than five people, yet according to the International Labor Office, they constituted between 30–50 percent of all employment in 1969. This enormous percentage shows the almost complete inability of existing economic systems to absorb the able-bodied population into regular employment.

According to the classification suggested by P. Hugon, it is possible to define female employment according to the following categories: domestic service, small-scale production (potter, seamstress, caterer, and food vendor), transport, and sales (mini-retailer, peddler, market woman, and authorized street hawker). To this cursory listing one may add, in the case of absolute pauperization, the work of women in Lima who belong to the lower levels of the underprivileged, work that consists of picking up garbage—gathering the scraps from the hospital kitchens and from the slaughter houses (Marie 1981). Last, one should include prostitution, as so many women live in miserable conditions that prostitution constitutes one of their major sources of income, either as a full-time occupation, or alternating with, or parallel to, other activities.

The rare studies devoted to these activities show that the proportion of women in the casual sector is equal to, if not often higher than, that of men: 63 percent in Argentina (Jelin 1982), 46 percent in Peru, and 53.3 percent in Brazil (Merrick 1976). The casual sector is flexible and many-sided enough to be able to employ women who must face significant economic responsibilities, whether they are young women, married women, or the heads of households. The correlation between the level of the family revenue and the necessity for paid work for women has been largely shown: in India, for example, 60 percent of the women belonging to families with a very low income (less than 100 *roupies* a month) work in the casual sector (Papola 1982).

Taking part in these activities are young women between fifteen and twenty-two years of age, still single, sometimes with responsibility for one or two children, often recent immigrants or living unmarried with someone (notably in Latin America), and whose companion also finds himself in a difficult situation because of illness, irregular and poorly paid work (for example, as an unskilled laborer or guard). Their income is so inadequate that in order to survive, all the members of the family—including the woman and often the children—must work. The multiplication of activities, poorly paid as they are, are a part of the strategy of survival. As one thirty-two-year-old Brazilian says: "I work too much, not because I like it, but because I have to. I support my family by doing a little bit of everything. I embroider, I sew, I paint, and during the night I make wooden objects, handicraft religious articles. I don't know how much I earn and I don't want to know, in order not to get really angry" (Cunha Neves 1980).

Another type of economic understanding prevails among couples in Africa: The man provides for some of the family's expenses, such as rent, water, transportation, and school costs, while the wife buys the food and the clothing, in this way reproducing the old sexual division of labor. "Food is the responsibility of the women even in the city. In the countryside they produced it directly, here (in Abidjan) she works in order to buy it" (Vidal 1977).

Finally, there are women who head households, who represent the only economic support for those nearest to them. A Brazilian study shows that 15.24 percent of these women find themselves in this situation because of a change in their matrimonial status (such as widowhood or separation). Fifty percent have to find work during their first union or marriage because the husband is unemployed or he contributes nothing to the support of the family, keeping his income for other uses (purchases of consumer goods such as a bike, a transistor, or presents for other women). This very frequent phenomenon shows how erroneous it is to consider the man as the head of the family "regardless of his contribution to the family budget" (F.I.B.G.E 1980). On the other hand, criteria defining the head of the family as "the person who is economically responsible for one or several dependents with whom they have ties of blood, conjugality or other," grant recognition to women's actual socioeconomic role and give them the place they deserve (Figueiredo 1980).

Admittedly, women solely responsible for their families are not yet in the majority. Yet in the large cities and even in the smaller ones, the conjugal tie has notably loosened. This is shown by the frequency of divorce and polygamy (with the more or less complete desertion of the first wife and her children, at least those up to ages six–eight). Rejection, recognition of the husbands irresponsibility, and the effects of economic depression—all these play a role as factors increasing the number of families in which a woman becomes the head of the household: commonly one-fourth of the families, in some cases one-third, in Nairobi and in Kenya, as high as 60 percent.

In Brazil, on the average a woman head of household devotes fifty-four hours per week to producing for the market. If one adds the time spent on unpaid domestic work, one arrives at an average of ninety-four hours of work each week, fourteen hours per day. Monthly incomes of female heads of households average less than those obtained by male heads of households: 72 percent of the women earn less than $90 each month, compared to 54.6 percent of the men. In New Delhi, a woman works forty hours a week for 76 *roupies* a month, while a man works for 192 *roupies*— which is to say that a woman, even though she is already working a double day, has to devote twice as much time as a man if she wants to earn as much.

Because of the undervaluing of and poor renumeration for women's work, the families with women in charge belong to the poorest group. In Belo Horizonte, Brazil, 27.4 percent of the families headed by men live below the poverty level (100 *cruzeiros* per person per month), but this percentage goes up to 44.9% for families having a woman at the head. Eighty-five percent of these women work in the casual sector (Merrick and Schmink 1978).

The statistics and studies that are beginning to appear concerning the role of women in the casual sector, although fragmentary, nevertheless clarify the living and working conditions of servants, peddlers, and prostitutes, as well as the specific ways in which they are exploited.

The inequality of urban incomes in the principal cities of the Third World has created a large market for domestic work. In Latin America, for example, the leading occupation of women is that of servant: from 1959–75, 45–70 percent of new employment for women was in domestic work (Arizpe 1981). This activity is almost exclusively a female preserve: in Mexico, 90.3 percent of the servants are women (Riz 1975). However, in Africa and Asia the concentration of women in this sector is less pronounced and the method of recruitment less restrictive, men being more frequently employed, except for the one well-known exception, South Africa.

It should be emphasized that this profession is, above all else, that of migrants who come into the cities with no skills other than those that they have acquired at home. Seven out of ten migrants in the Philippines become servants (Heyser 1981), and 91 percent in Lima, Peru. After having lived a few years in the city, these women try—or are forced—to leave this occupation. There is a correlation, therefore, between the length of urban residence, the age of the women (related to their childbearing period), and the occupation of household help. In 1970 in Buenos Aires, 51 percent of the migrants were servants, a percentage which fell to 35 percent among those who had five years residence (Ministerio de Trabajo, Argentina 1973).

Working conditions for the domestic workers mirror the level of economic growth, offering women greater or lesser opportunities for employment (outside of South Africa where the women are not allowed into the cities except for this work). The example of Singapore is typical: up until the 1970s and the intensification of industrial development offering new jobs, young servant girls were mercilessly exploited. Due to the ensuing competition, salaries rose, working hours were reduced, and weekends became free. Nevertheless, the acquired advantages risked becoming temporary, for they were not supported by any official legislation and remained tied to economic circumstances that might change at any time.

As a general rule, living conditions differ according to whether the servants live with their employer. In general, the "live-ins" are young women from fifteen–twenty-two years of age, often single or having no more than one or two children of their own. Since there is no protection for domestic work, these isolated women, with no unionization, are completely dependent on their employers, who can exploit them at will.

The salaries are very low: in Mexico, 87 percent earn less than 500 pesos a month, which is four or five times less than the legal minimum wage (Riz 1975). In Senegal, a servant earns in one year what an agricultural worker at BUD makes in one or two months (Kane 1977); in India, a female servant earns 40 roupies a month, which is three times less than a man earns (Papola 1982). But it is probably in South Africa that living and working conditions are the worst: "37 percent of African women in urban zones have a paid job. The majority are servants. No social legislation protects these workers, who are paid very low wages (the lowest are around 10 to 30 *rands* a month, [with 1 R approximating 1 U.S. $]). They have long hours, 12 or more per day, with usually one meal a day, a few weekends free each year. They live in a shed in the backyard of their employer and do not have the right to have even a very young child with them, not to mention their husband" (Emmanuel 1981).

The salaries are so low that one may wonder if they meet the need that represents the main reason for migration—the more or less complete support of the family remaining in the village. Actually the low urban salaries, in spite of everything, are still salaries that cannot be found in rural areas.

Nonetheless, even though the young women do not stay very long with their employers, this in no way affects the job market, since the labor reserve is so very plentiful. They leave for various reasons—weariness, refusal to have sexual relations with their employer, difficulties with their role as mother-wife, more pressing economic necessity, or another occupation. But having acquired no special skills in this period, they find themselves as unskilled and impoverished as before. Their possibilities are limited: if luck comes their way, they may turn into a factory worker, hawker, or prostitute for some years, or else simply revert to being a servant again, but on a part-time basis.

For example, in a shantytown located one hour by bus from Guayaquil, Ecuador, women become washerwomen. To do this, paying the bus fare, they have to go to the city to find clients, bring back the laundry, and wait for the water truck that brings water to the shantytown. This work, poorly paid by the piece, is unrewarding and fatiguing and is therefore only undertaken by women as a last resort. "There is surely something wrong in the household," the men say to themselves. For the most part it is a matter of a woman with no skills, who has been abandoned by her companion. In this shantytown, living together without marriage is standard practice, as is the instability of these unions, for there are seven women to one man (Moser 1981).

Under these circumstances it is possible to understand the enormous success of a television serial called *Simplemente Maria,* which, in the form of a story in pictures, has drawn a considerable audience among poor women, especially servants, in all the Latin American countries. It is the story of a dream. Its well-known social function is to neutralize revolt, and it is cleverly used by the image hucksters. "Born into a poor Indian family from the High Plateau, Maria leaves for the capital and begins to work at the bottom of the economic and social ladder: she is a servant. Her mistress treats her harshly. Seduced and abandoned by a medical student, a regular visitor to the family, she finds herself pregnant in these very difficult conditions. Then she meets a teacher who encourages her to learn sewing. Several years later she carves out a place for herself in the international world of Haute Couture and her life is elegant, rich and happy. . . ." (Newland 1979).

In numbers, the peddlers come right after the servants. In the city markets, in the streets, at entrances to factories, in front of their own houses, women of all ages practice commerce on a small scale—often with meager profits. They sell products that they have prepared (hot food, local drinks, dried fish) or grown (vegetables, condiments). More often, since it is rare that they have access to some small plot of land, they buy produce from a wholesaler and resell vegetables or fruits.

The number of women economically active or recognized as such in the commercial sector varies from one region to another and from one country to the next. Some live in extreme situations, such as the women recluses from northern India and northern Nigeria, who do not venture to the markets either to buy or sell (men and children take on these two roles). These women contrast sharply with women from Ghana who have almost all of the retail commerce well in hand: nine women out of ten in Accra are retailers. In West Africa, selling is without doubt the main activity of women: in 1970, in Ghana, 84.6 percent of the vendors were women, and in Senegal at Dakar more than 60 percent of the sellers at the market were women. The same is true in several other countries of Central and Southern Africa, such as Zaïre, Zimbabwe, Zambia, and Malawi.

In southern and eastern Asia, there are regions where women do the selling, and other regions where instead it is the men (Boserup 1970). Women represent more than half the work force employed in trade in Burma, Thailand, Cambodia, Laos, the Philippines, and Vietnam. On the other hand, in India this percentage drops to 11 percent with a difference between north (6 percent) and south (17 percent) because of the practice of female seclusion. In Latin America, female sellers are more numerous in regions where blacks and Indians predominate in the population, although these only represent 10 percent of the work force in the countries on the Atlantic coast.

Putting aside several isolated cases—the famous Mama Benz from Ghana [successful traders are nicknamed for their high-powered cars] or the powerful fabric vendors of Liberia—women are almost always concentrated in the sector of small retailing that is not very remunerative, but which is accessible to them due to the small amount of capital needed to start off. As to the men, they deal with wholesale commerce, where in general they are in the majority: for example, in Ghana, among the wholesalers there are eight thousand men to one thousand women. On the other hand, women work independently, going into business for themselves (84 percent in Ghana in 1970 and 24 percent in the modern commercial sector). Comparable data exists for Thailand (60 percent compared to 22 percent). On the contrary, in Latin America, the proportion of women employed in the modern commercial sector is much higher than the casual sector.

Time-consuming though it is, small trade provides such poor income that it often does not pay for the family's food. Retailers in

Java do not even earn enough to pay for the bus fare to and from the market. They go to the market every day, or four or five times a week, and stay there from six–ten hours. The work is exhausting and their earnings pathetic.

"Charles was dismissed from his work and unemployed for a whole year. Clementine was not going to abandon him in his misfortune. The purchase of a large tray, and of several dozen children's dresses is all it takes to start a small business . . . At the time the market opens in Adjame (Abidjan) at six A.M., she buys the dresses wholesale from the seamstresses, who have just arrived, then with the tray on her head, she leaves to resell the clothes in neighborhoods far from the market, in fact, hawking in the streets and the courtyards for hours. All the women know the prices and it is difficult to sell for a profit. Time has no great value in Abidjan and no one counts the time that Clementine has used in transporting her merchandise. Miles of walking earns her an average of 12,000 CFA Fr. a month, (at the time the minimum wage was 17,000 Fr.) the wherewithal to pay the rent (4,000 Fr.) and the food for the two of them. This kind of small commerce abounds and one could hardly imagine that it would disappear from the life of the common people, so much does it assure, at little cost, all of the distribution of highly essential goods" (Vidal 1977).

One can understand that sometimes very fierce competition develops between all these women who desperately need to earn a little money. These pressures reinforce a hierarchy based on the nature of the product and where the sale takes place. The situation of the woman who resells, installing herself in a busy street, or that of the roving vendor, is not comparable to that of women who obtain a place at the market and fight to keep it. For example, in Dakar, the fact that urbanization has a long history assures certain ethnic groups a de facto privilege of the best places. This privilege of an ethnic group or even of a family group is either guaranteed by a kind of right of inheritance or exemption from very high taxes (Le Cour Grandmaison 1979). This system evidently discriminates against migrants and new arrivals.

Being on their own, the women can hardly accumulate savings worth mentioning. There are some associations whose basic function it is to help women accumulate capital. Under different forms in a number of countries in Africa as well as on the island of Java, "tontines," that is, cooperative lotteries, provide women with access to a system of credit and savings, thus favoring the accumulation of a certain sum that they can invest in trade or in some other sector (repairing the house, buying some mode of transport, repayment of a debt, or, as on Java, buying earrings, for example, which can be pawned one day to facilitate another purchase). On Java, a tontine of 130 members functions according to a flexible system (Peluso 1981). The redistribution, which is proportional to the sum of the contribution, varies between 44,000 and 90,000 *roupies* every ten days. Those who pay 100 *roupies* every day receive 88,000 roupies; for 75 *roupies,* they will receive 65,000 *roupies;* and for 50 *roupies,* 44,000 *roupies.* Of course, given their number, the women do not benefit from this capital, but at the end of two or three months, their winnings can be thirty times higher than the income of a small vendor. Furthermore, women are affiliated with other smaller tontines, which provide a more modest sum of money with greater regularity.

The example of street restaurants furnishes a good instance of the difficulties that these women encounter when they have no access to credit organizations—which is most frequently the case. In Bombay, such women are in a special situation: on the one hand, their clients, who are for the most part temporary workers, members of the same "extended family" (from the same caste or the same village as the restaurant keeper), pay what they owe rather irregularly, which obliges the restaurant keeper to buy in very small quantities and often on credit from the local grocer. On the other hand, the relationship of dependence between the woman and *her* creditor can only deteriorate, given inflated interest rates (150 percent each year). As most of these women are illiterate (75 percent), or have very little education (17 percent have four years of school), the creditor is the one responsible for keeping the books. He has, therefore, all of the power: he forces the women to buy only from him and threatens to close their account and even forces them to respond to his sexual advances.

These restaurant keepers are hardly able to get out of this impasse, the more so because they are isolated and nonunionized. For their part, the unions consider these women as exploiters living off the workers by supplying them with poor meals at excessive cost. This blindness of the male-dominated unions shows up the outrageous distance between workers of the same class, but of different sexes. Nonetheless, in 1973, during a strike of forty-two days in the textile industries, the conduct of the women who fed the workers without compensation was exemplary: they even went so far as to put some of their own things in hock. This was noticed by one of the union members, who then tried to resolve the main problem and found them a credit union with very low interest rates (Savara 1981). The behavior that was judged to be exemplary was purely and simply a reenactment of a maternal function, this time applied to the sphere of work.

In the major cities of the Third World, where there are men living alone, where there are factories and workshops, where there are unemployed and poor, these women restaurant keepers are increasingly essential in assuring at minimum cost the maintenance of the work force, thus helping the state and the capitalistic enterprises avoid heavy social expenditures. They contribute also to maintaining a policy of low salaries, which constitutes one of the axes of dependence in the underdeveloped countries. But this use of the traditional sector has a limit: for example, the big plants employing more than a thousand workers are compelled to have a cafeteria (Rambaud 1981).

The profit margin for these women is very low. On the Ivory Coast, for a forty-seven–fifty-seven hour workweek, and depending on the type of dish that they make (grilled banana or rice with a peanut sauce) and their location (in front of the factory or in front of their own house), they earn varying amounts: 15 percent earn 10,000 Fr. a month, 68 percent earn from 10,000–20,000, and only 1 percent earn from 40,000–50,000 Fr. Another factor works towards lowering the profits: no matter how the prices fluctuate at the market, the women have to offer their product at an almost constant price, or they would risk a slump in their sales.

In spite of all the difficulties, one may say that this small-scale trading does offer women of all ages a meager, yet relatively stable, source of income. From this point of view the competition of manufactured products (pottery as opposed to plastic bowls and pails, or Marseille soap compared to local soap), whether of local origin or not, represents an immense danger for women, a threat that most development planners fail to take into consideration.

Prostitution is also one of the strategies for survival that women themselves, or their families, are led to adopt because of the increasing poverty of the rural milieu, the drying up of the labor market, and low salaries for women. Indeed, the incomes of washerwomen, waitresses, peddlers, and all those who live from these small trades, are not enough to pay for the support of a household, especially if a single salary must defray all expenses. For example, in a shantytown near Dakar, the rent for one small room, without water or electricity, represents one-fifth or one-fourth of the salary of a servant; all other necessary expenses cannot be paid out of the money gained from a single occupation.

Prostitution is then the most effective means of resolving a financial problem: in a lower-class neighborhood of Dakar where unemployment is endemic, by prostituting herself, one woman in one day can earn up to 500 CFA Fr. per trick, which is one-third, if not more, of the monthly wage of a servant. The supplementary income is often indispensable to manage other expenses like rent, school costs, repayment of loans, and medicine for relatives in the village.

The following two cases show how and why some women juxtapose different lives in the course of one day: a Senegalese woman, thirty-two years old, divorced, with three children to care for, is a cook and linen maid in a bar situated next to her house. She prostitutes herself whenever she can, for her income neither allows her to pay her rent nor the tuition charges of her two sons (her fourteen-year-old daughter is in charge of the house) (Savane 1978). A Thai woman of twenty works during the day on a poultry farm in Bangkok, where she earns twenty-five *bahts* a day [early in 1987, 26 *bahts* equaled one U.S. dollar], and she is a prostitute at night to support her parents and eight brothers and sisters who are in the country. "How can my salary go to pay my rent, my food, my transportation and the rest? And I can tell you that I economize" (Thitsa 1980).

Short-term economic reasons can also be decisive. At the time of the great drought of 1972–73 in the Sahel, nomadic women became prostitutes in order to survive in the shelter camps situated near the cities. "God does not look how you obtain money that you need to survive"—this remark by a Targui Moslem of the Niger shows that, even if in normal times prostitution is subject to rigorous social sanctions, in many cases it may be accepted when it is the only way to overcome destitution.

There are considerable differences according to country. In Africa, prostitution parallels the growth of cities and the male immigration that fuels that growth: prostitution applies especially to the native population and to other Africans who sojourn in the country. European tourism is more attuned to the slogan "sun, sea, sand, exotic cultures . . ." than to sex. European men praise the charms of African women, but the tour operators do not fill up their planes with single men searching for sexual pleasure, as do the tour operators specializing in the big cities of Southeast Asia. Nevertheless, around the large tourist hotels, the swimming pools, and the movie houses, some women try their luck. Here are the words of a woman interviewed in an inquiry labeled, *The tourists seen by those who serve them:* "I am a prostitute and I don't hide it. I do business with everyone, tourists or not. I have a price that varies between 5 and 10,000 Fr. for foreigners, and between 3 and 5,000 for Africans. . . . Each day I leave home at five o'clock in the afternoon and come back at seven in the morning. I live with my two children and my blind mother. I pay 6,000 Fr. a month for a room. I give money for the daily expenses—500 Fr. . . . It's the lack of family support that pushed me into this profession. I don't have any brother or sister and my father died young. My only source of income is my body. If I were a maid, I wouldn't even earn my bread, and I am not qualified to have a paying job elsewhere."

If the development of prostitution in Africa concerns mainly the African population in the big cities, the growth of prostitution in Southeast Asia (Thailand, Korea, and the Philippines) reflects a different evolution. In the latter area, the massive presence of the American army until the end of the Vietnam War changed everything. In 1974, in a single base in the northeast of Thailand, there were seven thousand prostitutes. This was followed by a specialty for tourists in terms of "sex voyages" organized by Japanese, German (Neckerman, Christoffel), or Dutch tour operators, for example. Prostitution became an export product and the object of a genuine economic policy. In 1977, Thailand welcomed 1,200,000 foreigners and twice that number in 1981. Tourism is the third source of foreign exchange for the country ($220 million), while rice brings $290 million and sugar $260 million.

The majority of the tourists are men—of the 200,000 Japanese visiting the Philippines, 87 percent were male; so were 81.7 percent of the 73,983 Japanese visitors in Thailand. These tourists are taken in hand by the tour operator, who, after an enormous publicity campaign, sells the trip with erotic pleasure included in the price (Thitsa 1980). One can read in the Frankfurt press about "Asiatic women, with no longing for emancipation, but full of a warm sensuality and the sweetness of velvet. . . ." One specialized German review explains that "in Bangkok men who have difficulties establishing sexual relations . . . can choose among hundreds of young women, who, for a small sum, will make him feel like a Don Juan." To accommodate them, "eros centers" have multiplied in Bangkok. According to the study of Dr. Thepanom of the University of Mahidal, there are 119 massage parlors, 119 hairdressing salons with massage and tea, 97 night clubs, 248 brothels, and 394 restaurants with a discotheque. In a salon, a pretty girl can earn sixty *bahts* an hour, a less attractive one, forty *bahts*. It is the "bound" girls who have been handed over to a recruiting agent by their parents to pay their debts, who earn the least. The clients are 50 percent foreigners, 30 percent Thai and Chinese businessmen, and 15 percent local civil servants.

A study dealing with fifty masseuses from nine establishments in Bangkok shows that they all were recent migrants belonging to large families; 56 percent of these families have five–seven children and are natives of the north (one-third) and the northeast (one-half), where a part of the population lives below the poverty level. Eighty-five percent of these girls, aged eighteen–twenty-three at their arrival in Bangkok, had emigrated for the purpose of contributing to the family income. They send a part of their earnings, about one-third, to their parents. Fifty percent earn between 3,000–6,000 *bahts* which represents a monthly salary 15–25 times higher than what they could earn from other occupations for women: domestic servant (150 to 460 b), waitresses (200 to 500 b), factory worker (200 to 500 b) *(Phongpaichit 1980)*.

What else
What else
Have you left me,
Heiress to your germs and your destruction?
Leave me,
The whore of the Embassy Hotel,
She weeps,
Hey, Joe, give me your dollar,
Not your napalm, nor your gonorrhea.
(Barhai Zain, Villariba 1981)

Servants, small retailers, prostitutes, millions of women, millions of families, succeed in surviving thanks to their disparate work; this women's work that is so little appreciated, so marginal, almost repudiated socially and economically, and quantitatively and qualitatively submerged in the abstractions of development.

6
From Hong Kong to Mexico: Women in Factories

INDUSTRIES IN THE COUNTRIES OF THE THIRD WORLD EMPLOY A large proportion of women between the ages of fourteen–twenty-four, and this proportion may run as high as 70 percent in some countries. Even if this figure represents but a very small minority of Third World women, in and of itself their employment in industry is a fundamental social and economic phenomenon.

At a time when male underemployment and unemployment prevail in that part of the world, why is it that women are employed at all? Why young women in particular? What sort of work do they perform and in what conditions? These are some of the key questions.

The history of industrialization varies according to Third World regions and countries. Indeed, it affects only a small number of countries in any significant way, about thirty of them in 1979. No more than six countries in Southeast Asia and in Latin America accounted for the bulk of industrial exports.

Underemployment and migrations toward the cities furnish an inexhaustible and inexpensive work force that becomes increasingly crucial as international competition more and more focuses on lowering labor costs. This sort of competition, linked to the growing structural crisis of the world economy, has reinforced the tendency to relocate, that is, to establish branches and sub-branches in the Third World. In this way, the electronics industry, which had established factories making components in the least industrialized zones of western Europe (such as southwestern France, Ireland, and Spain), no longer enlarges the existing plants, but, on the contrary, sets up new factories in certain Third World countries where labor costs remain much cheaper. Industry realizes two advantages in making such a move: one is achieved in terms of labor costs (through low wages), the other in terms of productivity (through a work speedup) (Salama and Tissier 1982; Gallez and Troupin 1980).

Wages in the export sector of the Third World will therefore be as low as economic, social and political conditions permit (Amin 1980). The proliferation of "free zones" must be understood within the logic of these pressures, exerted on multinationals and Third World countries alike. Above all, these are simply zones where labor laws are practically nonexistent. The employer's freedom to dispose of his labor force as he sees fit is further reinforced by the existence of authoritarian political regimes, military or civilian, with a tight control over that work force.

There is therefore a structural link, above and beyond the changing phases of the business cycle, between the growth of labor intensive industries during the sixties and the massive participation of women in the industrial work force—women who are always underpaid—which rose from 29.5 percent in 1970 to 40.1 percent in 1978. Within the Third World's industrial sector, women number 44 percent of the work force in Asia, 17 percent in Latin America, and 6 percent in Africa (International Labour Office 1981).

Such global figures conceal important differences, not only in terms of the countries involved, but also of the kinds of industry at stake. Women represent 39 percent of all workers in Singapore, for example, and 19.5 percent in Brazil; yet the figures are 31.1 percent and 69.4 percent respectively, in electric/electronic manufacturing, and even 64.3 percent and 84.6 percent in the garment industry of the two countries (Wong 1980).

Women work mainly in industries geared to the manufacture of products destined for the world market, such as textiles, clothing, sporting equipment, shoes, toys, furniture, wigs, watches, radios, television sets, and components for the electronics industry (like semiconductors, turners, valves). They also work in the chemical, pharmaceutical, and food and drink industries. In extractive and metallurgical industries, they are also present, though in smaller numbers. They constitute a majority in such cottage industries as cigar and lace making in Asia, embroidering in Mexico, and hammock making in Brazil.

The cottage industry, as well as industry within the framework of what is nowadays called the "Hong Kong Model," permits us to understand the mechanisms by which women workers are exploited. The analysis of these two situations puts into brutal relief the cultural stereotypes devaluing women. These stereotypes are utilized not only by the exploiters, but also accepted by the exploited, "justifying" the economic cynicism of the law of profit.

We have several studies available on the particular kind of

subcontracting based on women's domestic industry—the cigar makers and the lace makers of India. Three common characteristics emerge:

1. The products made by these women are most often destined for an international market and for consumers of developed countries, but the industries are, for the most part, owned by local capitalists.

2. The women engaged in this type of remunerated work come, without exception it seems, from the poorest rural social classes—from those living below the poverty threshold.

3. With minimal differences, the same organization prevails everywhere. A contractor distributes the raw materials to the women through a network of agents and intermediaries, who then return for the finished product. The advantages for the exporter are obvious: he has no investment in the fabrication, in machines or any other equipment, and no difficulty in adjusting supply to demand (if need be, no raw materials are distributed to certain women). Managing and controlling labor is facilitated by the isolation and dispersion of the women workers among different villages, as well as by the poverty which traps and maintains them within a system of indebtedness and of almost total dependence.

The fabrication of *beedi,* the local name for cigarettes smoked by the poor, but also very popular among American women, is concentrated in the region of Allahabad in central India, which has been Moslem since the tenth century (Bhatty 1980). The population is made up of two groups: the Ashrafs and the non-Ashrafs. The Ashrafs, converted earlier, are hierarchically superior, forcing their women into complete seclusion and exclusion from all economic activity. The non-Ashrafs are poorer and, considering the practice of seclusion as evidence of a higher status, have always tried to follow that pattern. Whenever they are able, their wives, who usually hire themselves out as farm laborers, prefer to work at home, even though it means lower incomes. In this way, and with full backing of their husbands, they hope to attain the more prestigious life-style, an aspiration not to be underrated given their economic and social destitution. The need for dignity can overshadow the need for food.

In 1974, the Indian Ministry of Labor estimated the number of workers in manufacture of *beedi* to be 2.5 million, of whom half a million worked in existing factories. Of the two million home workers, 90 percent were women belonging to the caste of Untouchables or from among the landless or the very smallest landowners, that is to say, from among the most poverty-striken social groups. Indeed, the plots of land at the disposal of these people are so inadequate, that they provide no more than 0.2 percent of the total family income.

Therefore the main source of income for this population, 70 percent of whom live below the poverty level estimated at 51 *roupies* per capita and per month in 1978–79, is agricultural wage labor for the men and the fabrication of *beedi* for the women, aided by their children. On the average, women contribute 45.5 percent of the family income, and amongst the poor the figure may rise as high as 85–95 percent. In working 6.89 hours per day during 285 days in a year, on the average a woman earns 845 *roupies*. In 1966 and 1976, two laws tried to regulate this sector of production, notably by imposing a minimum piece work rate, but without success.

The lace makers live in the region of Narsapour, India, where poverty has continued to increase since the beginnings of the Green Revolution in 1961 (Mies 1980). Rice sells at too high a price for the poor to purchase, for the number of agricultural workers earning less than the legal minimum has grown 10 percent between 1961–71. This pauperization forces women and children to do any kind of work to help the family survive.

The region of Narsapour has played an important role in textiles since the beginning of the seventeenth century until the time—around 1813—that England opened India to competition from machine—made fabrics. Around the same time, missionaries made their first converts among the Untouchables (the Harijans). The Harijan women learned lace making and crocheting, skills that were unknown until then. After the great famine of 1896–97, two brothers set up a regular lace export business. They orgainzed the business using women agents to distribute thread and patterns to the lace makers and to pick up the finished product. The growth of this industry, which has been substantial since the 1960s, has benefited not only from increasing poverty, but also from the desire of the women from the Untouchable caste to work at home.

The development of the lace industry since the 1950s is underlined by the increasing number of countries that are importing local lace: Australia, the Netherlands, Denmark, Sweden, Canada, Great Britain, the Gulf Emirates, Norway, Belgium, West Germany, and others. Around 1966, as a consequence of the Green Revolution that brought sudden prosperity to substantial landowners, the increasing wealth of these farmers led them to invest, notably in commerce and still more, in lace, where production costs were so low that they allowed very rapid accumulation. In order to become an exporter, all that was required was the address of an importer, in addition to having some patterns and agents to distribute thread to the women. These new merchants utilized men in place of women, not only as agents, but also as skilled workers, assembling the different designs that the women had crocheted at home. Ever since that time, the market has been controlled by men.

The annual production of lace is estimated at ten million *roupies* in 1978, a figure which represents 90 percent of the amount made by handicrafts production in that state. It is, however, very difficult to know the exact number of lace makers, who may number two hundred thousand. Indeed, this is not the only paradox: the census that so clearly describes the cottage industry—in which all work is done by women—does not count them among "active workers" on the pretext that they make lace "for their own pleasure."

It is therefore supposedly to fill their leisure time that such women put in about eight hours' work a day, making the same design over and over again. They earn forty *roupies* for each twelve dozen designs, corresponding to forty-five thousand feet of thread transformed into lace. The agent takes his cut of 10 percent of the wages paid by the employer. A woman can work up sixty-five hundred feet of thread in the course of one week. She will earn a daily salary of 0.56 *roupies,* whereas the minimum wage for agricultural labor is 3.4 *roupies* for men and 2.25 *roupies* for women. The income of the lace maker has remained stationary since 1931, but this "stability" has not, one may assume, applied to the consumer goods she has to buy.

The work day of a lace maker, including paid and unpaid labor, is approximately fifteen hours per day. If a woman were also able to devote the seven hours she spends on housework to lace making, she would still earn only a wage of 1.40 *roupies* a day, at a time when the minimum subsistence income is estimated at 1.60 *roupies.* To get an idea as to what is involved, a sari costs between 30 and 70 *roupies.*

Ridiculously low as they are, in 50 percent of the cases women's wages are indispensable for their families' survival. Unaided, the men simply cannot manage alone. Compared to the woman's contribution, on the order of 23 percent of the family income, that of the man is obviously larger, yet not because he works longer hours. On the contrary, the men work only eight hours a day during six months of the year, while the women work fifteen hours a day for twelve months. What makes the difference is that men's work is better paid. In six months, a man earns 900 *roupies* and a woman only 90 *roupies*.

In a real sense, no one wants to face this undervaluing of women's work. This probably accounts for the author of the census monograph on the cottage industry permitting himself, without the slightest shame, this idyllic description of the lace makers' work:

> Usually in the afternoon women from two or three neighboring houses get together on their front porch and begin to make lace, all the while talking amongst themselves. Thus this industry has the social effect of bringing neighbors together. In this way, the leisure time of the women serves to earn money that they can profitably use for themselves or that augments the family income. (Mies 1980)

This aspect of the cottage industry's "pleasant family atmosphere" disappears completely when it comes to the anonymous quality of factory work. Asia has experienced an unparalleled growth of its exports. In the case of South Korea's exports, for example, the share of manufactured products went from 14 percent in 1960 to 88 percent in 1976. These exports involve mainly fifty-four categories of products made by a preponderantly female work force. Shipments of toys multiplied by 3 between 1970–76, hosiery by 4.8, garments by 6.5, recording and hi-fi equipment by 40.8, and watches by 34.6.

Workers are young: 73.2 percent are from 20–24 years of age in Singapore; in Taiwan 46 percent are between 15–19, and in South Korea 35.5 percent are between 14–19. Their professional life lasts about ten years (Ahooja Rata 1981) because in the process of exploitation their workday is lengthened and their work pace speeded up: they are rapidly driven to exhaustion. This pattern is accentuated enormously in the free zones. Kaohiung in Taiwan, for instance, employs 70 percent women, of whom 50 percent are under 20 years of age. It should be noted that for 59 percent, this is their first job.

What are the reasons for this infatuation with a female labor force? Most certainly it does not reflect the unavailability of male labor, since a large number of men remain unemployed. Neither is it a matter of distributive justice, tipping the scales to equalize women's opportunity for paid work. Capitalist firms recruit their work force on the basis of profitability, not social idealism. Theorists who have considered this problem are in agreement that this predilection for a feminine work force rests on the economic, social, and political certainty of employers that they have the power to exploit these women systematically and with complete impunity (Elson and Pearson).

Female work is paid at lower rates, while being more productive. Salaries are 20–50 percent lower than those for men doing the same work (Kreye 1977), with the exception of electronics workers in the free zone of Penary, Malaysia. It has to be recognized that to compare the productivity of men and women is all the more difficult in that very few men are employed to do the skilled assembling done by women. Nevertheless, at the request of the Malayan government, two multinational firms have tried to give this type of work to men (Lim 1978). The experiment was a failure, as the men were less productive.

The high productivity of women is not their only quality. Firms and governments seeking to attract foreign investments affirm that there is a "natural" difference that makes women more dextrous, more agile, more docile, and more inclined to accept strict work discipline. One example of advertising shows how consciously the feminine appeal is utilized:

> the manual dexterity of Oriental women is extolled the world over. Their hands are small, they work fast, but very carefully. Consequently, who is better qualified by nature and by inheritance to contribute to the efficiency of assembly production than an Oriental young lady? The salary rates in Malaysia are among the lowest of the region and women workers can be hired for about $1.50 U. S. dollars per day. (*Far Eastern Economic Review* 1979)

There is also the instance of a Haitian in charge of an electronics plant, who, in an interview on French television, explained with some smugness, that, in contrast to the United States, women in his country were content to repeat the same movement twenty-five thousand times a day, and that women in great numbers wanted to be hired for this kind of work (Télévision française I 1982).

If a differentiation between men and women as workers really exists, it is by no means natural, but derives "from the way male and female roles are socially construed" (Elson and Pearson 1980). The young women's nimble fingers are not a biological heritage like the color of their hair, but the result of their experience within the family as young girls. Some of their skills, such as sewing and knitting, are transferable to the assembly operations going on at the factory:

> . . . manual dexterity of a high order may be necessary in the typical operations of piecework, but, nevertheless, these operations can usually be learned rapidly thanks to the traditional skills. It takes six weeks to learn how to make factory-made garments for girls who already know how to sew. (Sharpston 1976)

It has been demonstrated that jobs identified as women's work are most often classified as semi-skilled or unskilled, while jobs technically similar, but identified as men's work, are classified as skilled jobs. (Phillips and Taylor 1979). The jobs reserved for women in electronics are considered unskilled not for technical reasons, but on the basis of beliefs and prejudices that happen to be singularly advantageous to employers. Evidence in support of this are the aptitude tests that would-be female employees must pass with high scores. Employers choose women because they learn fast and therefore become highly productive very rapidly. This problem must be recognized in any study on the work of women.

Over and above this "natural" training, schooling is equally appreciated. Thus, "contrary to a narrow and excessively pessimistic view," preference is given, especially in the free zones, to young girls who have gone to school, because they take more readily to factory discipline (Salama and Tissier 1982). The literacy rate in the six countries of Southeast Asia with a large industrial sector exceeds 71 percent. Literacy, which has always been the basis for women's liberation, may in certain circumstances be used to accentuate their dependence. Some companies, for this reason, stay in touch with the principals of secondary schools.

The immutable regularity with which women's wages are lower than those of men is attributed to their "second-rate status" in the labor market. As a matter of fact, it is currently admitted that women cannot raise children at the same time as acting as chief providers for their family. Their salary is therefore presented as an "additional" salary, an "extra," a vague "over and above" without which, let us repeat, the very poorest, that is, one billion two hundred million people in 1972, could not survive. The hypocrisy is striking, for even women who are heads of household—women who have been abandoned, or are single, widowed, divorced, or married to unemployed men—continue to receive this salary, amputated by one-third or one-half compared to male wages. As for young girls, they do not need to receive a higher salary since they are not married, and because they leave their work when they become pregnant. Before marriage or after, women are always penalized for their biological ability to bring children into the world.

In the free zones in Asia, not only does the unskilled female work force receive wages one-tenth as high as its counterpart in developed countries, but, moreover, 34 percent of women compared to only 15.6 percent of men earn less than $200 a month. The following table shows clearly the sexual discrimination in incomes:

Monthly Income in Dollars by Sex
and by Training, 1978
(*Yearbook of Statistics, Singapore* 1978)

	Men	Women	Difference
Never attended school	342	200	142
No training	348	200	148
Primary schooling	334	221	113
Post–primary schooling	276	227	49
Secondary schooling	405	315	90
Post–secondary schooling	568	437	131

Statistics are also available regarding other countries. According to the International Labor Bureau, in Sri Lanka, for instance, monthly salaries amounted to $31 U.S.. In Malaysia, more than one-third of the women workers leaving the rural areas find wages of less than $2 a day. These low wages are paralleled by considerable insecurity of employment, because the multinationals, in response to fluctuations in the world market, unpredictably adjust their work force by layoffs and firings (notably for pregnancy). To this must be added the very difficult working conditions that lead to premature aging and many illnesses.

In Taiwan, the export industries—garment, leather, T.V. sets and other electronic equipment—comprised 56 percent female employees and 17 percent men. The work week was forty-eight hours on the average, with only seven paid holidays. Toward mid–1977, 85 percent of the employees of plants in the free zones of Taichung, Kaohiung, and Nantze were women. Of a total of 56,800, 6.1 percent were from 14–15 years old, 40.4 percent from 16–19, and 31 percent from 20–24. They worked eight–twelve hours a day, six days a week, for $60.

In the Philippines, women often work without a contract and are paid by the piece, a method that lowers salaries still further. Young women are considered apprentices as long as possible or else temporary workers, which makes it possible to pay them less than regular workers. In Bataan we found a young woman hired in a garment factory who learned her work in less than a day, but remained as a trainee for three months, during which time she received only three-quarters, that is, $20.60, of the minimum wage of $27.50. From this income, she sent 35 pesos to her family, using 109 pesos for her current expenses (20 for lodging, 45 for food, and as much for transportation, clothes, and other items).

There is also the matter of legal minimum wages, something that South Korea lacks altogether. Officially, the average monthly salary was $151 yet in American or Japanese electronics plants it was only $108, whereas it was estimated that minimum subsistence required $118. In November 1976, a woman employed in a thermometer factory in Seoul worked 30 days a month, from 8:00 A.M. to 8:00 P.M., for 22,000 *won*, which amounts to about $45. From this she paid 5000 *won* for rent, an expense she shared with her sister; 13,000 for food; 7000 for water and electricity; and 2,100 for transportation. In the Philippines, the average salary of a woman worker is $54–$67, while the expenses for food and transportation amount to $56. Even though the Thai government had fixed a minimum salary of 25 *bahts,* certain foreign firms did not meet this minimum. Several of these companies in the highly skilled sector went even further in demanding that the minimum wage be abrogated and that the minimum working age be lowered to fifteen. The average pay for unskilled woman workers is $37.50.

Added to these miserable salaries that barely permit survival are some fringe benefits which are also very low and that may be suspended arbitrarily for disciplinary infractions. As a matter of discipline, a woman worker loses her benefits by being between one and four minutes late three times. (In one factory a woman stopping work because of a skin condition, dizziness, or nausea from acid fumes is fined $8.15.)

Working conditions are such that accidents are numerous: disability cases have multiplied by 2.7 between 1970–76. (Korea Herald 1977). In the Philippines, 61.6 percent of the declared accidents led to temporary total disability, though we do not have data listed according to sex. Nevertheless, we do know that women contract many illnesses. Those who work in the textile industry suffer from back ache and varicose veins (Pearson 1978); those using microscopes in electronics ruin their eyesight in two or three years (Grossman 1978); others are exposed to skin disease, vertigo, or nausea from the acid fumes and from solvents; finally, they are subject to fatigue and the general deterioration of their health, a situation made worse by being confined to one working position (Heyser 1978). As soon as a woman becomes less productive, she is dismissed. She has to find a new way to survive, something that is so difficult that prostitution is often the only recourse.

The implacable exploitation of this work force is seen very clearly when one studies the various concessions granted by Asian governments in the hope of attracting foreign investors to the free zones: teams of three women workers compelled to work standing up are authorized; night shifts are also allowed. In Thailand exemptions are granted for work "that must be carried out by continuous shifts" or work which, by its very nature, must be done at night (*International Labour Office* 1972), in the Philippines for the tasks requiring the skill and manual dexterity of women (*International Labour Office* 1974), or in Indonesia for jobs that by their nature, their location, or the special circumstances in which they are carried out, must be performed by women (*International Labour Office* 1955). Firms are often exempted from paying social security taxes. As for maternity leaves, the women need not worry, for pregnancy is a cause for dismissal.

In the tariff-free zones, special privilege is king. During the prolonged state of siege proclaimed by the Marcos regime in the Philippines in 1972, the Ministry of Labor was authorized to sign a warrant for the arrest of any person accused of subversive activities. This reinforced the restrictions limiting the power of unions. Sunday was no longer an automatic holiday, and firms could make their personnel work seven days in rotation without having to pay overtime. In general, the political and social rights of workers were suspended. An extreme case is that of Singapore, where numerous women from Malaysia are employed under contract. These workers are forbidden to settle there permanently, to change their jobs (yet if they happen to be out of work, they are expelled), or to marry save after five years' residence, and then only with the consent of the government and an agreement that husband or wife will undergo sterilization after their second child.

Finally, it is necessary to say a few words about the policy of stretching out the workday, a policy applied systematically, but by different means: by a system of demerits in the shoe factory of Dae Sang Op Co. in the zone of Masan, South Korea—demerits based on supposed employee inadequacies in the areas of sincerity, cooperation, efficiency, attendance and loyalty; a point system in the Hankuk Iwatami Company, where the slightest tardiness or the refusal to work overtime are penalized by five demerit points. In Korea, certain enterprises have their workers come in thirty–forty minutes early and keep them thirty–forty minutes after the official quitting time, a practice that adds one-and-a-half hours of unpaid labor. Another firm has removed mirrors and wash basins to lessen time spent in the restrooms.

The juxtaposition of a fixed wage and work paid by the piece also allows lengthening the work time. That is what is done in the Seoul, Korea, garment shop, *Peace Market*. To make a complete outfit, four workers are needed: a tailor, a tailor's aide, a woman machine stitcher, and her female aide. The stitcher alone is paid by the piece and must make a certain quota each day, regardless how long this takes. This obliges the aide, who is paid by the month, once she herself is "finished," to put in unpaid overtime until the piece work quota of the stitcher is met. In Singapore, many women workers put in eleven–twelve hours per day, which at the end of the month comes to a certain number of hours of overtime, only part of which are paid, thanks to such practices of "nibbling" the working hours. In Korea, the weekly forty-eight hours may be carried to sixty if the work contract permits it. Rest breaks during these extremely long and tiring days are not paid. The South Korean woman worker will work 268 days a year, the equivalent of 2,144 hours, overtime not included, in comparison to a French woman worker who will put in about 1,840 hours.

As soon as women were drawn into factory work in Latin America and in Africa, it assumed the same characteristics: a youthful work force, low wages, sexual division of labor, and discrimination. A study of sexual division of labor in Brazil (Hirata 1981) makes it possible to show how similar the mechanisms underlying the utilization of a feminine work force really are.

In Brazil, the participation of women in the work force went from 17.9 percent in 1960 to 32.6 percent in 1978. Women's employment tripled in manufacturing industries, while that of men only doubled. This increase marked the entrance of women into the dynamic industries, such as certain sectors of metallurgy, and the production of electric and electronic equipment. Until that time, women had been confined to those branches traditionally considered female. This change in the structure of the work force was brought about by a policy of integration and association with international capital that led to the "economic miracle" [a decade of very rapid industrial growth], through policies initiated after the overthrow of the democratic, populist government in 1964. Until the recent restoration of democracy, Brazil had the combination familiar in Asia: a strong military regime, the development of consumer goods industries with foreign capital (the proportion of foreign capital in manufacturing is 82 percent), and an increase in the number of women workers (19.5 percent in 1976).

In Brazil, the reasons for recruiting women are the same as those discerned in Southeast Asia and, to a lesser degree, in France and throughout the world (Kergoat 1982). These reasons are, first of all, tied to the nature of the work, which is identical to domestic labor: monotonous, repetitive, meticulous tasks, but often dangerous within the factory setting. For example, the woman who has to produce some cylinders of paraffin by melting that paraffin without the benefit of a thermometer, knows that paraffin becomes an explosive at a certain temperature. The reasons are also tied to the productivity of women. In the words of Brazilian industrial managers, they go "faster," they have "a natural aptitude," they are "patient," and "they work fifteen to twenty times faster than male workers in other branches." In short, they resign themselves to poor working conditions. The reasons are also tied to their lack of combativeness. They "demand less," they accept dismissals more easily, and they are "submissive, disciplined, and do not create problems. When it is time to leave, they say 'ciao' and they go."

By making these points about the family, social, and economic environment of women workers, the Brazilian example allows us to get at quite another problem. All of the women, whether they are married, living with someone, or alone with the children—even young girls, though to a lesser extent—face the fact that after their outside work they must put in another day's work of domestic tasks for which they receive no pay. Given the conditions of extreme poverty of much of the urban population, they often take on still a third "day," this time paid, such as sewing, ironing, or other paid labor they perform in their own home.

The mobilization of women in Brazilian industry and elsewhere has taken place without any change in societal conditions: there are few day nurseries (33 nurseries provided by private firms and 122 neighborhood nurseries in São Paulo; that is, 9,000 places for one million children), few baby-sitting facilities, few laundromats, schools, and inadequate community transportation. One woman

works in a team on the factory floor from 5:00 A.M. –1:30 P.M.,
then from 1:30–4:30 P.M. in the staff kitchen. At home she
washes and irons the uniforms of the factory football club and the
linens from the staff restaurant (napkins, tablecloths, and towels),
which provides her with a supplementary income of 2,000
cruzeiros per month, an addition to the 8,000 *cruzeiros* she earns
working in the plant. After finishing this paid work at home, she
sews some skirts for her coworkers at 100 *cruzeiros* per skirt. Her
husband and two sons, twenty-seven and sixteen years old, do
nothing around the house: "my husband lies on the sofa and
there is no point to bawling him out." Another woman, who "gets
one hour off for lunch, returns home to get lunch for her seven-
year old son. Her salary of 7,000 *cruzeiros* a month does not allow
her to take the bus four times a day and, living twenty minutes
from the factory, she runs every day both ways. She has thirty-six
minutes to prepare the meal. . . ."

The low salaries that force women to double up on their work
and speed up their work pace in turn increase their nervous
tension and fatigue, accentuating thereby their sense of being
inferior professionally. With rare exceptions, every hierarchical
organization entrusts all skilled jobs to men. Women, therefore,
are always controlled and supervised by men in a climate of sexist
insults and sexist oppression. Added to this is the phenomenon of
job sex discrimination, as well-known in our own countries as in
the Third World: in Brazil a male lathe operator made 50,000
cruzeiros in 1969; a female lathe operator of similar skills earned
only 13,000; and this occurred in economic circumstances charac-
terized by one of the highest inflation rates in the world.

The picture that we have just painted is gloomy. When a cen-
tury-and-a-half after the onset of the industrial revolution in
Europe, we witness the exact reenactment of conditions in
women's work that accompanied nascent European industrialism,
it makes one question the meaning of words like "progress" and
"development" that are used so glibly. Here is what M. Guilbert
writes concerning female textile workers at the beginning of the
nineteenth century:

> Women's wages, as a general rule, amount to 50% of those of men.
> The employment of women and children becomes the favored
> method of reducing manufacturing costs. . . . Working hours depend
> on the employer's wishes, as no regulations intervene. . . . Inasmuch as
> they are doing the simplest tasks, they are more easily replaceable,
> hence accept more readily the most disheartening jobs. . . . Every-

where industrial concentration makes heavy demands on a female work force. . . . In the terrible waste of manpower that marks the earliest development of large-scale industry, women, together with children, are those most harshly exploited. (Guilbert 1966)

At that time the indignation and denunciation that this exploitation provoked contributed to forcing governments, concerned that their country's very labor pool would dry up, to draft labor legislation intended to protect women. Yet at present, in the countless conferences, roundtables, seminars on development, North–South dialogues on equalizing terms of trade, who has spoken out against the enslavement, the subhuman living conditions, of this female labor force?

Without wishing to be unrelentingly pessimistic, one may nevertheless wonder what upheavals will be needed to break the power of the multinationals, allied to national elites. In the meantime, the countries of the Third World, considering their demographic growth and the extreme youthfulness of their population, do not even worry about their future labor supply. Those showing concern would risk losing some newly established industrial plant. The scale on which industrial relocations are taking place, something eminently contemporary, provides transnational enterprises not only with geographic mobility, but with flexible ethics. This will permit them to take advantage of growing world poverty for some time to come, able to find, somewhere, both a docile government and a pliable work force ready to cater to their demands. This is the underlying meaning of the proliferation of free zones where lawlessness is the law of the land.

Conclusion: Common Denominators

WOMEN FROM AFRICA, SOUTH AMERICA, OR ASIA ARE ACQUAINTED with the same working conditions; they experience the same difficulties and the same rebuffs, despite differences in their societies, their religions, and their cultures. There are numerous similarities, but we shall focus on those that are the most illuminating, those which allow a coherent and dynamic reading of the processes that structure their lives.

Unifies

First of all, their ability to reproduce is an obvious common denominator. This is what defines women as a specific human group, the foundation of the social fabric, yet a group that is especially vulnerable. Medical data demonstrate that the health of mothers is threatened.

The gross birth rate is high, varying from 45.6 per thousand inhabitants for Africa to 43.4 for Asia and 38.8 for Latin America, compared to 16.2 per thousand in industrialized countries. According to the World Health Organization, in some countries 50 percent of the mothers have their first child before they have reached the age of twenty, and their precarious condition raises the chance of fatal mishaps (World Health Organization 1981). Rates of maternal mortality of five hundred per one hundred thousand live births are frequent. In some regions of Africa these mortality rates exceed one thousand (compared to European rates between five–thirty). In Africa, as well as in western, southern and eastern Asia, where the mortality rates are highest, each year 500,000 women die from accidents linked to pregnancy and childbirth, leaving about one million children motherless. We should note that the much lower rates furnished for Latin America are unreliable, for several studies have demonstrated that there is a serious underreporting of maternal deaths.

These deaths occur for many reasons, including postpartum hemorrhage, where anemia is often the initial or associated cause, blood poisoning, or hypertension. There are also too many pregnancies that are too closely spaced, especially as they affect women who are either too young or somewhat overage for easy childbearing. In this connection, we should mention how extremely rare deliveries handled by qualified personnel really are: 3 percent in Asia, 6 percent in Africa, 12 percent in Latin America.

Maternal mortality is accompanied by a high rate of infant mortality. Despite progress realized in this domain, in Africa one child in four is liable to die before reaching adolescence and sometimes it is as many as one in two. Every year twelve million babies die before reaching the age of one year. "Infant mortality, Jesus Maria! In a small burg like this that has one hundred houses, two children die every day. Every day there is a wake for some child, yes, every blessed day" (Conceiçao 1981).

Here again the causes are tragically simple: the poor health and the poor nutrition of the mother results in too low a birth weight. (Twenty-one million children weigh less than 4.9 lbs.) The babies' chances of survival are thereby diminished. Their risk of dying is twenty times that of an adult. In this exposed situation, the child is subject to tetanus (representing 10 percent of the deaths among newborns), diarrhea, and respiratory infections. Malnutrition is part and parcel of this pathological situation and intensifies it: malnutrition may be responsible for up to 57 percent of all infant deaths between the ages of one month and one year: the mother's lack of milk, with consequent poor nutrition due to family poverty, is usually at fault (Puffer and Serrano 1973).

Once more we are confronted by poverty and hunger, accentuated by development policies—both agricultural and industrial—geared toward exports, widening the gap between demographic growth and food production. During the 1960s, 56 of the 128 developing countries underwent a rate of demographic growth exceeding that of food production per inhabitant. During the seventies, this figure rose to sixty-nine including heavily populated countries like India, Pakistan, Mexico, and Egypt. The first to be affected are pregnant women, nursing mothers, nurslings and young children, all of whom have special nutritional needs: two-thirds of the women in the Third World are anemic; 54 percent of the children of landless families suffer from protein deficiency. There are also other deficiencies, notably involving vitamin A which causes blindness—50,000–100,000 children go blind each year from malaria affecting the cornea; 200 million have endemic goiter (Food and Agricultural Organization 1977).

The prevalent malnutrition among women and children calls for a few comments relating it to the economic and cultural order. Changes in the systems of production brought about by the development of a market economy have increased the number of hours worked by women. In some countries women have been obliged to abandon high energy food crops that required too much labor for less nourishing staples. Elsewhere the pressure of time has led them to prepare food less frequently—no more than one hot meal per day—and/or in some different way. All this affects the whole family's diet (Food and Agricultural Organization 1979). Yet there is a time-honored custom on three continents that directly influences women's diets: the obligation to serve the men first and to give them the best part of the meat, fish and sauce, the sources of proteins and lipids.

In urban zones, the decline in nursing also plays an important role in infant malnutrition. This is caused by the increasing participation of urban mothers in the work force with no social programs to assist them. It is also accentuated by the publicity downgrading mother's milk in favor of replacement products. For the most part, mothers in these countries lack the money, the know-how, or the kitchen utensils needed to prepare a baby bottle that would be safe. Their children have to swallow a diluted and polluted mixture with poor nutritive content, but abounding in bacteria. The triple combination of infectious diarrhea, serious malnutrition, and oral moniliasis fungus resulting from this is often fatal (King 1966). Data available from India, Chile, and other regions of South America indicate that among children raised on the bottle, the mortality rate is much higher. On the other hand, the economic cost of replacement milk bought in adequate quantities corresponds to 50 percent of the minimum wage in Tanzania and Kenya. Elsewhere it may eat up the entire salary of a woman on low wages.

The Nestlé's lawsuit (Nestlé is the second largest producer of foodstuffs in the world, with 299 plants scattered throughout the globe—95 of them in developing countries with a total yearly gross of over two billion dollars) exposed and denounced that company's commercial and advertising strategies: posters throughout cities and distributed in hospitals had been announcing, "Raise your baby with love and Lactogen," "Lactogen makes for strength and health"; similar publicity was aired on the radio; free samples were distributed. Much as these methods were castigated, the verdict could hardly have been more lenient. The moral criteria condemning such propaganda were largely ignored. Since that time, the World Health Organization has worked out an international code dealing with the selling of replacement products for mother's milk. Yet the results are disappointing. Within one year some two thousand violations had already been reported from thirty-seven countries. What can the deaths of hundreds of thousands of children mean for these multinationals that have reached a level of detachment and power that we can hardly gauge—for whom profit is the sole motive?

The poor health of women and babies is worsened by deplorable living conditions in the absence of all hygienic amenities. Only a small number of them have access to safe drinking water and the possibility of getting rid of excreta safely. The rest drink more or less polluted water. Yet the link between drinkable water, plumbing, and the reduction in various forms of diarrhea has been demonstrated by numerous studies. According to a report on countries with a per capita gross national product below $150, only 18 percent of the rural population of India, 1 percent in Ethiopia, and 12 percent in Zaire enjoy safe drinking water (World Bank 1980).

A second feature that all women have in common is the place of housework and the lack of recognition it receives. This has to do with men (as fathers and husbands), with statistics (that figure women among the "inactive"), with national economic accounting (where women's contributions, however fundamental, are omitted from the gross national product). This illogical attitude possesses a logic all its own, unjust as it may be; it also simply displays a lack of realism and common sense. As the tip of the iceberg, this attitude points to a host of blind reactions in the face of a dangerous social situation. Such omissions allow essential aspects of women's contributions to be ignored. Economically and culturally, therefore, their status is impoverished and undervalued. They end up as negligible social actors; indeed, they become "extras." As this peasant union member from northeastern Brazil describes,

Washing the laundry, cooking, sweeping the house, taking care of the children, all this is never considered work. There is something nonsensical about this, for at home one spends all one's time working. . . . When the men go out to work the land with their wives, the women work as hard as the men do. Then they come home. . . . Do you think that the husband will ever lift a finger in the kitchen? Never! He goes out to talk to the neighbors or he takes a shower. Then he installs himself in his hammock or in a chair. As for his wife, she starts all over from scratch. She washes everything, prepares everything for the next day, but that's not considered work. Yes, these things have to be done, but that's women's work. Save for a few exceptionally nice guys, where in the countryside can you find the father of a young child willing to stay with the baby when the mother is busy? And suppose the little pig pees or soils itself? Now that, never! To clean up a baby! A man? Clean up the shit of one's own kid? No, but . . . the mother has to rush over. That's her work. Men have nothing to do with that. (Conceiçao 1981)

A comment of this type is extremely rare, but expresses forcefully the double burden that women must carry. Reliable recent studies show that many women have fifteen–sixteen-hour work days. The examples that we have cited throughout this book have shown rural and urban women subjected to an exhausting daily life, a daily life that society reduces to nothing. To pound millet for hours, to carry over many miles water and wood that weigh as much as sixty pounds, to prepare meals while worrying about not having money and where the next meal is coming from, to think about errands that have to be run, to watch a sick child, to fret about the speedup at the plant and the gift that will have to be bought for a sister's wedding . . . In fact, in this daily living that is so undervalued, women reveal themselves as superb managers of their time, a shattered time, split into productive and housework hours. "To deal with the problem of time is to grasp how the social mechanisms of oppression and exploitation mesh, reinforcing each other during every day, every week, and throughout the entire life of a woman worker" (Kergoat 1982). This is true for all working women.

At home, in the fields, and in the factory, women do the monotonous, repetitive, and finicky tasks that men refuse, but which women accept in order to earn a little of that money needed to help their family survive. They have a keen sense of their own responsibility in this area, a sense that, it has to be noted, many men fail to share. In many social settings, the men control all of the money, their wives' earnings as well as their own. Women have to hand over what they have to pay for their man's drinking and smoking, for the purchase of his watch or bike, or for his trip to Mecca. A lot has been said about the destruction of relationships, about "the destabilization of family roles" (Daune-Richard 1982), but much less—is there some fear of committing sacrilege?—of the increasing and distressing irresponsibility of men in their roles as husbands and fathers. Besides, in a great many families, the husband is completely absent. Forty percent of Latin American households are headed by women; in Chile, 43 percent of all women fifteen years or older are mothers living alone (Buvinic and Yussef 1978). How many women in Asia and Africa have assumed such roles without having been counted? It is enough to talk to those in charge of urban social services in Africa to be convinced that there are more and more women experiencing complete material and psychological distress (World Bank 1979a). The sequence of desertion is all too well known: the woman is taken in marriage, abandoned, replaced, and left to her own devices. This is the tragic treadmill of masculine irresponsibility, miring the men in poverty and reinforcing that of their women.

Like some chemical reaction, a curious amalgam of objectivity, prissiness, and formalism takes over whenever the vital necessity for women to receive a salary equal to that of men is brought up. Yet such a salary would merely be a salary of dignity, in short, an adequate salary, rather than the so-called "supplementary wage." Once again women are saddled with the unrewarding task of denouncing the undervaluation of their work, permitting their increasing exploitation in the Third World. Nevertheless, it is necessary to bring this phenomenon to light. Such undervaluing perpetuates poverty and, by so doing, perpetuates child labor, thereby subjecting children to systematic exploitation. In these conditions of inequity and economic dependence, it perpetuates high birthrates as well. Poor families and poor women need children, who then become the trump card in the group's elaborate strategies for survival. By migrating and becoming wage earners, some of them fit themselves into the capitalist economy in order to bring home some income. Others engage in subsistence farming, while still others, the girls, will stay at home to help their mothers. Having received less schooling than their brothers, they in turn will become active agents in perpetuating a system of oppression that has already victimized their mothers.

The poor family does not merely procreate thoughtlessly, as some like to say, but from necessity. The structural conditions of poverty create a chain of exploitation, linking the father to his young daughter: in order to augment earnings, the number of people must be augmented, something which the enthusiastic proponents of birth control often forget. As long as the poor remain poor, they will continue to have children, who represent for them an indispensable hope of an easier life and an easier old age. The family planning programs with their distribution of birth control pills and intrauterine devices have been, are, and will remain ineffectual, in spite of the billions of dollars spent, as long as women remain uneducated and are unable to earn a decent living. For a long time the fact has been acknowledged that the birth rate goes down only after income rises: natality in low-income economies ($150 per year) is 46.6 per thousand per year as against 16.2 per thousand in industrial countries, where the average annual income is $5950. Any drop in the rate of population growth is contingent upon women's access to employment and decently paid work.

From time immemorial, conditions for women seem to have been such that, with rare exceptions, they have been excluded from economic, as well as from political and social, power. They have been kept out of the arena of public discussion. The weight of this segregation is obviously overwhelming. The inferiority of women serves as the foundation for a complex of ideological constructs the effectiveness of which correlates with women's degradation. Women are victims of a constant reversal of values, so that anything with which they are associated takes on a negative connotation. Biologically motherhood sets them apart, ethically their impurity isolates them from the world, metaphysically their very being is guilty, and the great religions agree in condemning them: in Christianity they are linked to original sin; in Hinduism an evil life is punished by reincarnation as a woman.

Over the centuries, women, submitted to this incessant and many-sided indoctrination, have had no choice but to internalize these cultural models that largely condition their lives. They are offered only a single path to redemption and that is through work, yet it is work that involves self-denial. The fact is that women are held in subordination as daughters, wives, mothers, or workers, whether paid or not (Institute for Development Studies 1979). And in all its aspects, their condition entails their domination by men. Endangered pregnancies and undervalued labor are the two traits of women in the Third World that underlie necessary subjection, assuring their docility. Take the Congolese peasant who is persuaded that her husband will become ill if he carries the loads of sixty-five–ninety pounds that she carries almost every day over several miles; take all those who consider it their duty to take on a double workday; take those who believe that the discrimination of which they are the victims is in the very nature of things.

Thus a woman is responsible for any task that is considered of no account, and thus she is in charge of nothing. She is therefore exploitable and punishable by her family, her husband, her father, or her employer. She is eminently expendable in her fertility, as in her work. She is employed when young, rejected once she has had children. She is without a future and without prospects.

All this, which is hardly new, is made worse by the living conditions within the cities and metropolitan areas which are the lot of an increasing number of women. One has to ask oneself how these women, alienated from their own nature, made to feel inferior, derided by everyone, will be able to carry on their essential task of educating and socializing the young. What image of herself will a woman be able to project to her children, and what image of their mother does society convey to these children? If the same pitiless forces continue to dominate relations between the northern and southern hemisphere, between the industrialized and the under-developed world, the social disintegration which has begun and which we are witnessing—for instance, the selling of children particularly of little girls as workers or prostitutes by parents reduced to such expedients in order to survive—will go much further than our good conscience allows us to imagine. A new kind of slavery is in the process of being created. To drive women to despair on such a massive scale is to create a fundamental danger of dehumanization.

In spite of this "structural violence," to which women are forced to submit by patriarchal institutions and so-called economic laws, women everywhere do try to find ways of coping. The specific content of these struggles provides a final similarity. Trade union-ism is rarely the route women take; although more and more of them do join unions, they are rarely among the activists. This is not merely from lack of time, but also because the battles unions fight often ignore their real needs as producers and reproducers. Finally, women are invariably excluded from their decision-making process.

When women organize, it is more likely to be on the basis of freely chosen small groups, based on neighborhood, kinship, or other like criteria. One example is, the women beer brewers, all of them heads of households, who have joined forces to the point where they constitute an entire neighborhood of Nairobi; or con-sider Congolese women cooperating by taking turns working in each other's fields helping each other with certain difficult, time-consuming and urgent tasks like mounding; or take the shan-tytowns of Guayaquil, where women, upon the birth of their first child, join an organization called "co-mothers" (just as one speaks of "co-wives" in a polygamous society), whose function is mutual aid in baby-sitting, in order to free up enough time for work. Women also fight side by side with their men, as in the case of the wives of Bolivian miners who have created the Committee of Housewives of the Twentieth Century in order to obtain better living and working conditions (Barrios de Chungaras and Viezzer 1976).

One should emphasize the emergence of another phenomenon which, in the long run, constitutes perhaps the most active social ferment. Among the poorest, the most deprived, the most socially marginal women—for example, among the casteless of India—women, who, moreover, as heads of households or as wives, are in fact economically responsible for the welfare of their families, a new consciousness of the contradiction between their own reality and the patriarchal ideology is beginning to emerge. Even if they are not yet rebelling, they do understand that they are being exploited. They are aware that their work alone—their devotion, their imagination, and their mastery of everyday problems make possible their family's and children's survival. They know intuitively the ferocious and illusory discrepancy between the value of men and women that social discourse sanctions. They know that they constitute "the strength of the weak" (Henry 1975).

Yet these struggles, this courage, this will to live and to assure life will only change things, people, and events to an infinitessimal degree, as long as women remain enmeshed in this net that ideology and culture have fabricated and that the capitalist economy exploits so cold-bloodedly. It will not be enough finally to begin a North–South dialogue that would recognize women's fundamental role in the construction of a more humane society. It will also require a political will on the part of the nation-states to alleviate poverty and destitution among millions of human beings.

Work has been the key word, the leitmotif of this book, its obvious focus and its rationale. Yet within the reality that we have described—a description conditioned by Western experience—the abstract concept of labor is almost completely alien to the cultural environment of women.

The notions by which our own Western societies analyze work—in terms of labor force, working class, hours of labor, and work pace—come out of a series of struggles that have resulted in a work ethic whereby the worker has conquered the right, one of many, to intervene in the conditions of production. Ever since the Industrial Revolution, a long effort of cultural reflection on the part of theoreticians and workers has permitted workers to challenge and redress their subordination to employers, and even exercise a certain degree of control over their working conditions. Third World societies have borrowed this ethic, where, more or less in the same form, it may be found among workers educated by union struggles, whether in Latin America, Asia, or Africa.

Yet women wage workers know almost nothing about this slow conquest of the workplace by the workers themselves. Indeed, throughout this book, we have shown how the different forms of their employment are generally based on their ignorance, which, in turn, permits a more intensive exploitation. Their ignorance has become a factor of production.

For women, work is an even more alienating experience than it is for men, because the very notion of alienation, of being estranged from one's basic human nature, is, and remains, beyond their reach. The capitalist world has insulated women so that they have remained unconscious, yet their isolation is also supported by the traditional attitudes of their fathers and husbands. Ignorance is the result of a dual economic and cultural coercion that converges to keep women docile within the labor structure. Imprisoned as they are by their own culture and ignorant of other cultures, the oppression to which women are subjected takes place at every level: their work—both biological and economic—constitutes, at one and the same time, their condemnation and their redemption. In this way, the alienation of women workers differs fundamentally from that of men.

References Cited

Agarwal, B. 1981. *Agricultural Modernization and Third World Women: Pointers from the Literature and an Empirical Analysis.* World Employment Programme. Research working paper. Geneva: International Labour Office.

Ahooja Rata, R. 1981. *Working Women in Asia. The Three Immobilities.* World Employment Programme. Research working paper. Geneva: International Labour Office.

Altamir, Oscar. 1978. *La dimension de la pobreza en Americana Latina.* Santiago del Chile: Comision Economica para America Latina (CEPAL).

Amin, Samir. 1980. "Développement auto-centré, autonomie collective et nouvel ordre économique et international. Quelques réflexions." *L'Avenir industriel de l'Afrique,* edited by Amin Sadir, Alexandre Faire, and Daniel Malkin. Paris: L'Harmattan.

Amselle, J.-L. 1976. "Les Migrations africaines. Réseaux et processus migratoires." Amselle, J.-L., *Dossiers africains.* Paris: Maspéro.

Arizpe, L. and J. Aranda. 1981. *Empleo agroindustrial y participation de la mujer en el desarrollo rural, un estudio de las obreras del cultivo de exportacion de la fresa en Zamora, Mexico.* World Employment Programme. Research working paper. Geneva: International Labour Office.

Barrios de Chungara, Domitila and Noëma Viezzer. 1976. *Si on me donne la parole. La vie d'une femme de la mine bolivienne. Témoignage recueilli par Noëma Viezzer.* Paris: Maspéro.

Bessat, C. and J. Trouvé. 1982. "L'exode rural des jeunes et les politiques de développement, l'expérience camerounaise," in International Labour Office, *Phénomène migratoire et politiques associés dans le contexte africain.* Geneva: International Labour Office.

Bhatty, E. 1980. *Economic Role and Status of Women: A Case Study of Women in the Beedy Industry in Allahabad.* World Employment Programme. Research working paper. Geneva: International Labour Office.

B. I. R. D. 1980. *Health Sector Policy Paper.* Washington, D.C.: World Bank.

Bisilliat, Jeanne. 1982. *Les femmes rurales au Congo dans les districts d'Abala, Kindamba, Mindouli (région des Plateaux et du Pool).* Mission Report. Rome: Food and Agricultural Organization.

Boserup, Ester. 1970. *Woman's Role in Economic Development.* London: Allen and Unwin.

84

Buck, J. 1976. "Report presented within the framework of the consultative group on proteins and calories," in Food and Agricultural Organization, *Les Femmes et la production alimentaire, la manutention des aliments et la nutrition.* Rome: F.A.O.

Burbach, R. and P. Flynn. 1978. "Agribusiness Targets Latin America." *NACLA Report on the Americas* 12 : 2–33.

Buvinic, M. and N. Youssef. 1978. *Women-headed Households, the Ignored Factor in Development Planning.* Washington: International Center for Research on Women.

Les Cahiers français. 1974. Editorial. "La leçon des expériences. Les limites de la révolution verte." Direction de la documentation française. *Les Cahiers français* 167 : 16.

Chonchol, J. 1982. "Une nouvelle politique agraire ou l'explosion sociale." *Le Monde diplomatique* 29 (September): 15–16.

Collier, W. I. 1975. *Agricultural Technology and Institutional Change in Java.* Agricultural Development Council, staff paper, no. 75-1.

Conceiçao, M. da. 1981. *Cette terre est à nous. La vie d'un paysan du Nordeste brésilien. Récit recueilli par Ana Maria Galano.* Paris: Maspéro.

Connell, John and B. Dasgupta. 1976. *Migration from Rural Areas. The Evidence from Village Studies.* Delhi: Oxford University Press.

Cunha Neves, Angela. 1980. "Femmes et développement au Brésil," *Revue Tiers Monde* 21: 893–98.

Daune-Richard, Anne-Marie. 1982. "Sociologie du développement ou développement de la sociologie: la question des femmes et de leur travail." *Revue Tiers Monde* 23: 375–87.

Deere, C. D. and M. L. Leal. 1980. *Women in Agricultural Peasant Production and Proletarianization in the Three Andean Regions.* World Employment Programme. Research working paper. Geneva: International Labour Office.

Dozon, J.-P. 1977. "Economie marchande et structures sociales: le cas des Bété de Côte d'Ivoire." *Cahiers d'Etudes Africaines* 17: 463–483.

Dupire, M. and J.-L. Boutillier. 1958. "Le pays adioukrou et sa palmeraie (Basse Côte d'Ivoire), Etude socio-économique," in *L'Homme d'Outre-Mer.* Paris: O.R.S.T.O.M.

Economic and Social Council/Food and Agricultural Organization. 1974. *The Role of Women in Population Dynamics Related to Food, Agriculture and Rural Development in Africa.* Addis-Ababa: E.S.C./F.A.O.

Eglin, J. and H. Thiery. 1982. *Le pillage de l'Amazonie.* Paris: Maspéro.

Elizaga, J. 1970. *Migraciones a las aràs metropolitanas de America Latina.* Santiago de Chile: C.E.L.A.D.E.

Elson, D. and R. Pearson. 1980. "The Latest Phase of the Internationalization of Capital and its Implications for Women in the Third World." Discussion paper. Institute for Development Studies, University of Sussex.

Emmanuel, D. 1981. "La femme noire sous le régime de l'Apartheid." *Jonction 5.*

Far Eastern Economic Review. 1979. (18 May).

Fiéloux, Michèle. 1980. *Une étude socio-économique dans la région de Damba (Sénégal).* Mission report. West Lafayette, Indiana: Purdue University.

Figueiredo, Maria. 1980. "Le rôle socio-économique des femmes chefs de famille à Arembepe (Brésil)." *Revue Tiers Monde* 21: 87–91.

Food and Agricultural Organization. 1960. *Recensement mondial des terres.* Rome.

Food and Agricultural Organization. 1977. *Fourth World Food Survey by the F.A.O.* Rome: F.A.O.

Food and Agricultural Organization. 1979. *Les femmes et la production alimentaire, la manutention des aliments et la nutrition.* Report of the United Nations' consultative group on proteins and calories. Rome: F.A.O.

Fundação Instituto Brasileiro de Geografia et Estatística. 1980. *Anuário estatístico do Brasil.*

Gallez, A. and J.-L. Troupin. 1980. *Les pays en développement de l'Asie de l'Est et du Sud-Est dans la perspective d'une nouvelle division internationale du travail.* 2 vols. Louvain: Université de Louvain.

George, Susan. 1976. *How the Other Half Dies. The Real Reasons for World Hunger.* Harmondsworth, U.K. and New York: Penguin Books.

Ghai, Daram, Eddy Lee, and Samir Radwan. 1979. *Rural Poverty in the Third World: Trends, Causes and Policy Reorientations.* World Employment Programme. Research working paper. Geneva: International Labour Office.

Gosselin, Gabriel. 1978. *L'Afrique desenchantée.* vol. 1: *Société et stratégie de transition en Afrique tropicale;* vol. 2: *Théorie et politique du développement.* Paris: Anthropos.

Grossman, R. 1978. "Women's Place in the Integrated Circuit." *Pacific Research* 9: 2–17. (Joint issue with *Southeast Asia Chronicle* 66.)

Guilbert, Madeleine. 1966. *La question des femmes dans l'industrie.* The Hague: Mouton.

Henry, P.-M. 1975. *La force des faibles.* Paris: Editions Entente.

Hewitt de Alcantara, Cynthia. 1976. *Modernizing Mexican Agriculture: Socio-economic Implications of Technological Change, 1940–1970.* Geneva: UNRISD.

Heyser, N. 1978. "Young Women and Migrant Workers in Singapore's Labour Intensive Industries." Paper presented at Conference on the Continuing Subordination of Women in Development Process. Institute for Development Studies, University of Sussex.

———. 1981. "Towards a Framework of Analysis," in "Women and the Informal Sector." *I.D.S. Bulletin* 12. Brighton, U.K.: University of Sussex.

Hirata, H. 1981. "Division sexuelle du travail et role de l'Etat: l'exemple brésilien," in *Le travail des femmes. Critiques de l'Economie Politique* 17. Paris: Maspéro.

Hugon, P. 1982. "Le secteur non-structuré dans les villes du Tiers-Monde," in *Les grandes villes africaines*. Séminaire de Montpellier. Paris: Ministère de la Coopération et du Développement.

Institut tricontinental. 1982. *Famines et pénuries: la faim dans le Monde et les idées reçues*. Paris: Maspéro.

Institute for Development Studies. 1979. Special issue on the Continuing Subordination of Women in the Development Process. *I.D.S. Bulletin* 10, 3, University of Sussex.

International Labour Office. 1955. *Legislative Series*. Part 1, Indo. 1. Geneva.

———. 1972. *Legislative Series*. Thai. 2. Geneva.

———. 1974. *Legislative Series*. Phi. 1. Geneva.

———. 1981. *Femmes au travail*. Geneva.

———. 1982. *Phénomène migratoire et politiques associées dans le contexte africain*. Geneva.

Jalée, Pierre. 1973. *Le pillage du Tiers-Monde*. Paris: Maspéro.

Jelin, E. 1977. "Migration and Labor Force Participation of Latin American Women: the Domestic Servants in the Cities." *Signs* 3: 129–41.

———. 1982. "Women and the urban labour market," in *Women's Roles and Population Trends in the Third World*, edited by R. Anker, M. Buvinic, and H. Youssef. London: Croom, Helm.

Journet, O. 1981. "La femme diola face au développement des cultures commerciales," in *Femmes et Multinationales*, edited by André Michel. Paris: Karthala.

Kane, Francine. 1977. "Femmes prolétaires du Sénégal." *Cahiers d'Etudes Africaines* 15 : 77–94.

Kelkar, G. 1981. *The Impact of the Green Revolution on Women's Work Participation and Sex Roles (India)*. World Employment Programme. Research working paper. Geneva: International Labour Office.

Kergoat, D. 1982. *Les ouvrières*. Collection actuel. Paris: Le Sycomore.

King, M. 1966. *Medical Care in Developing Countries*. Nairobi and London: Oxford University Press.

Kinley, David. 1982. "Quand le "progrès" aggrave la misère paysanne." *Monde Diplomatique* 29 (November): 19.

Korea Herald. 1977. (20 July).

Kreye, O. 1977. "World Market Oriented Industrialization of Developing Countries: Free Production Zones and World Market Factories." Working paper.

Kurian, R. 1981. *The Position of Women Workers in the Plantation Sector in Sri Lanka*. World Employment Programme. Research working paper. Geneva: International Labour Office.

Le Cour Grandmaison, Colette. 1979. "Contrats économiques entre époux dans l'Ouest africain." *L'Homme* 19 : 159–170.

Lim, L. 1978. *Women Workers in Multinational Corporations in Developing Countries: the Case of the Electronics Industry in Malaysia and Singapore.* Occasional paper No. 9, Women's Studies program. Ann Arbor: University of Michigan.

Linhart, Robert. 1982. *Le sucre et la faim.* Paris: Editions de Minuit.

Loufti, M. F. 1980. *Rural Women: Unequal Partners in Development.* World Employment Programme. Research working paper. Geneva: International Labour Office.

Marie, Alain. 1981. "Marginalité et conditions sociales du prolétariat urbain en Afrique. Les approches du concept de marginalité et son évolution critique." *Cahiers d'Etudes Africaines* 21 : 347–74.

Merrick, T. W. 1976. "Employment and Earnings in the Informal Sector in Brazil: the Case of Belo Horizonte." *Journal of Developing Areas* 10 : 337–54.

Merrick, T. W. and M. Schmink. 1978. "Female-headed Households and Urban Poverty in Brazil." Working paper. Belmont, Md., conference: "Women in Poverty: What Do We Know?"

Mies, M. 1980. *Housewives Produce for the World Market: The Lace Makers of Narsapour.* World Employment Programme. Research working paper. Geneva: International Labour Office.

Ministerio de Trabajo, Argentina. 1973. *Condiciones de la familia migrante con especial referencial al rol de la mujer.* Buenos Aires: Ministerio de Trabajo.

Moore-Lappé, Frances and Joseph Collins with Cary Fowler. 1977. *Food First. Beyond the Myth of Scarcity.* Boston: Houghton Mifflin Company.

Moser, Claus. 1981. "Surviving in the Suburdios," in "Women and the Informal Sector." *I.D.S. Bulletin* 12. Brighton, U.K.: University of Sussex.

Newland, K. 1979. "L'image d'elles." *Forum du développement* (March).

Palmer, Ingrid. 1977. "Rural women and the basic needs approach to development." *International Labour Review* 115 : 97–107.

Papola, T. S. 1982. "Sex Discrimination in the Urban Labour Markets: Some Propositions Based on Indian Evidence," in *Women's Roles and Population Trends in the Third World,* edited by R. Anker, M. Buvinic, and H. Youssef. London: Croom, Helm.

Pearson, R. 1978. "The Mexican Border Industry: A Case Study of Female Employment in Modern International Industry." Paper presented at Conference on the Continuing Subordination of Women in the Development Process. Institute for Development Studies, University of Sussex.

Peluso, N. L. 1981. *Survival Strategies of Rural Women Traders or a Woman's Place Is in the Market. Four Case Studies from Northwestern Sleman, the*

Special Region of Yogyakarta. World Employment Programme. Research working paper. Geneva: International Labour Office.

Peru, Direccion National de Estadisticas y Censos. 1965–68. *Encuesta de Immigracion Lima Metropolitana*. Reports 1, 2, 3. Lima: Direccion National de Estadisticas y Censos.

Phillips, D. and B. Taylor. 1979. "Sex and Class in the Capitalist Labour Process." Working paper presented to the Conference of Socialist Economists (London).

Phongpaichit, P. 1980. *Rural Women of Thailand from Peasant Girls to Bangkok Masseuses*. World Employment Programme. Research working paper. Geneva: International Labour Office.

Prosterman, R. L. 1979. "La colère des sans-terre." *Forum du développement* 58 (November–December).

Puffer, R. R. and C. V. Serrano. 1973. *Patterns of Mortality in Childhood*. Scientific publication no. 262. Washington, D.C.: Panamerican Health Organization.

Rambaud, C. 1981. "La restauration de rue dans les zones industrielles et tertiaires modernes d'Abidjan." Working paper.

Raymer, S. 1975. "The Nightmare of Famine." *National Geographic* (July).

Riz, L. de. 1975. "El problema de la condicion feminina en America Latina; la participacion de la mujer en los mercados de trabajo. El caso de Mexico," in Comision Economica para America Latina. *Mujeres en America Latina*. Mexico City: CEPAL.

Roldan, I. M. 1981. *El caso de las trabajadoras del tomate en el estado de Sinaloa, Mexico*. World Employment Programme. Research working paper. Geneva: International Labour Office.

Rullant, Denis. 1982. "Brésil: la fin de vivre." *Actuel Développement* 49:23–27.

Salama, P. and P. Tissier. 1982. *L'Industrialisation dans le sous-développement*. Paris: Maspéro.

Savane, Marie Angélique. 1978. "La prostitution en Afrique." *Famille et Développement* (Dakar) 13:13–23.

Savara, M. 1981. "Organizing Annapurna," in "Women and the Informal Sector." *I. D. S. Bulletin* 12. Brighton, U.K.: University of Sussex.

Shaheed, F. 1981. *Migration and its Effects on Women in the Village of Provenance*. World Employment Programme. Research working paper. Geneva: International Labour Office.

Sharpston, M. 1976. *International Subcontracting*. Oxford Economic Papers.

Silva de Rojas, A. E. 1981. *Effectos del empleo de mano de obra feminina en la industria de las flores: un estudio de caso en Colombia*. Seminario tripartito regional para America Latina sobre el desarrollo rural de la mujer. World Employment Programme. Research working paper. Geneva: International Labour Office.

Singapore Government Printing Office. 1978. *Yearbook of Statistics.*

Stamp, Patricia. 1975. "Perceptions of Change and Economic Strategy among Kikuyu Women, Mitero, Kenya." *Rural Africana* 29 : 19–44.

Télévision française 1. 1982. "Les larmes amères du soleil haïtien." 3 September, French television program, channel 1.

Thitsa, K. 1980. *Providence and Prostitution. Image and Reality for Women in Buddhist Thailand.* September 1980. London: Change.

Traoré, A. 1981. *L'accès des femmes ivoiriennes aux resources. Les femmes et la terre en pays adioukrou.* World Employment Programme. Research working paper. Geneva: International Labour Office.

United Nations. 1980. World Conference on the United Nations' Decade of the Woman: Equality, Development, and Peace. Copenhagen, 14–30 July 1980.

Vidal, Claudine. 1977. "Guerre des Sexes à Abidjan. Masculin, féminin, CFA." *Cahiers d'Etudes Africaines* 17 : 121–53.

Villariba, M. C. 1981. *The Philippines: Canvasses of Women in Crisis.* London: Change.

Wong, A. 1980. *Economic Development and Women's Place. Women in Singapore.* London: Change.

World Bank. 1979a. *La femme dans le développement, une inconnue que la Banque Mondiale apprend à découvrir.* Washington, D.C.: World Bank.

World Bank. 1979b. *World Atlas of the Child.* Washington, D.C.: World Bank.

World Health Organization. 1981. *Vers un avenir meilleur: la santé maternelle et infantile.* Geneva: W.H.O.

Young, K. 1978. "Economia campesina, unidad domestica y migracion." *America Indigena* 38 : 279–302.

Index

Abidjan (Ivory Coast), 38; peddlers in, 53; sexual division of labor in, 48

Accra (Ghana), 52

Adioukrou: economic relations among the sexes of, 33–34, 36, 38–39; palm plantation economy among, 33–34, 36, 38–39; social impact of palm oil processing plant on, 36

Africa, 14, 15, 20, 22, 25–26, 30, 31–45, 48–50, 52–53, 56, 60, 76–77, 80–81; Abidjan (Ivory Coast), 38, 48, 53; Accra (Ghana), 52; Adioukrou, 33–34, 36, 38–39; agricultural society and women's roles, 30–32; apartheid, 20; Banileke women (Cameroon), 35; Bete (Ivory Coast), 35–36; Bud Company (Senegal), 25–26; Cameroon, 41–42, 43, 44; Central Africa, 32, 35; coffee growing among Kikuyo, 39–40; commercial farming, impact of, on women and marital relationships, 34–36; Congo, 31, 32, 39, 80; co-ops, women deprived of access to, 39–40; credit, women deprived of access to, 39–40; Dabou (Ivory Coast), 36; Dakar (Senegal), 25, 42, 52, 53, 55, 56–57; Diola women (Senegal), 35, 37; domestic service, 49–50; Egypt, 75; Ethiopia, 14, 77; Gambia, 32; Gbeye women (Central Africa), 35; Ghana, 37, 45, 52; infant mortality, 75; Ivory Coast, 33–34, 35–36, 38–39, 53, 55; Kenya, 14, 22, 39–40, 44, 76, 81; Lagos (Nigeria), 43; Lesotho, 14, 43, 44; Liberia, 52; Malawi, 44, 52; Mali, 25; Mama Benz (Ghana) 52; migrants' remittances, 44–45; migrations by women, 41; Nairobi (Kenya), 48, 81; Nigeria, 14, 45, 52; peddlers in Abidjan (Ivory Coast), 53; peddlers in Accra (Ghana), 52; poverty, 14; prostitution, 56; Sahelian countries, 56; Senegal, 25–26, 32, 35, 42, 44, 45, 50, 52, 53, 55, 56–57; sexual division of farm work, 32; sexual division of labor, 48; Société d'aménagement et d'exploitation du delta (Senegal), 32; SODEPALM (Ivory Coast), 38; South Africa, 22, 49, 50; southern Africa, 52; Tanzania, 14, 76; Targui Moslems, 56; Upper Volta, 39, 43; West Africa, 52; women in industry, 60; women's household tasks, 33; women's rebellion against male dominance, 35–36; Zaïre, 52; Zambia, 52; Zimbabwe, 52; Zinguinchor (Senegal) 42

Agro-business: Bud Company (Senegal), 25–26; Garcia Enterprises, Sinaloa (Mexico), 27; in Sabana region (Colombia), 27–28; in Sinaloa, state of (Mexico), 26–27; in Zamora valley (Mexico), 28–29

Agro-industrial complexes, Third World, 18

Alienation, 83

Allabahad (India): cigar makers in, 61–62

Anderson, Clinton P. (U.S. secretary of agriculture), 18–19

Anemia, 75

Apartheid, 20

Argentina: casual work sector in, 47, 49; domestic service in, 49

Ashrafs (India), 61

Asia, 14, 16–18, 21–25, 38, 41–50, 52–55, 57–58, 59–64, 67, 69–71, 75, 78, 80, 82; Allabahad (India), 61–62; Ashrafs (India), 61; Bangkok (Thailand), 43, 57, 58; Bangladesh, 14, 22, 43; Bataan (Philippines), 68;